MERLENE TARVER HOWARD

Through the
BIBLE
in Rhyme

10530409

Through the Bible in Rhyme

Printed in the United States of America.

PROMINENT
BOOKS EDGE

5830 E 2nd St, Ste 7000 #9983
Casper, WY 82609
USA

To my family and friends who have a dream, go for it.
See it can be done.

CONTENTS

Genesis

The Beginning.. 3

Adam and Eve.. 4

Eve Listened 5

Cain and Abel.. 6

Methuselah.. 7

Noah 8

The Rainbow 9

Babel 10

Abram and Lot 11

Abram and Sarai.. 12

Lot.. 13

Father Abraham 14

Abraham's Seed 15

Isaac's Wife 16

Ishmael 17

Jacob and Esau 18

Jacob's Ladder.. 19

Jacob Wrestled God 20

Jacob's Wives 21

Joseph 23

Joseph, the Slave.. 24

Topman.. 25

A Family Reunited.. 26

The Twelve Tribes.. 28

Exodus

A New Generatio (Exodus) 33
Baby Moses 34
The Burning Bush 35
Moses 36
Pharoah's End 37
Have You Heard the Story? 38
The Amalek War 39
God's Mercy Seat 40

Leviticus

Sacrifices Unto God 43
Eating Holy Things 44
I Am Your God 45

Numbers

Numbers 49
Milk and Honey Land 50

Deuteronomy

The Defeat of Og 53
Ten Commandments 54
Fear the Lord 55

Joshua

Joshua 59
Cross Over Jordan 60
Rahab 61
The Walls Fell 62
Secret Sin 63
Joshua's Death 64

Judges

Judges 67
God's Women 69
Gideon 70
God Gets Angry 72
Samson 73
Samson's Wife 74
Samson and Delilah 75

Ruth

Naomi and Ruth 79
Ruth and Boaz 80

1 Samuel

Hannah 83
Samuel Grew 84
The Ark of God 86
Samuel Judged 87
King Saul 88
Saul Messed Up 89
David is Chosen 91
David and Goliath 92
Run David Run 93
David and Abigail 94
The Death of Saul 95

2 Samuel

King of Judah 99
Michal 100
David's House 101
David and Bathsheba 102

Nathan's Parable.. 103
Absalom's Conspiracy... 104
Absalom... 105

1 Kings

Solomon Made King 109
Solomon's Wisdom 110
God's House... 111
Queen of Sheba... 112
King Solomon's Death 113
Jeroboam 114
Kings 115
Run, Elijah, Run 116
The Widow... 117
Angry Jezebel 118
Naboth's Vineyard... 120

2 Kings

Elijah and the Fifty.. 125
Elijah's Whirlwind... 126
Naaman 127
Good News 129
Death of the Witch 130
Elisha's Death 131

1 Chronicles

The Record 135
David's Army 136
A Warrior Messed Up 137

2 Chronicles

Solomon—Son of David 141
A Magnificent House 142
When the Queen Came 143

Ezra

Building the Temple... 147
The Finished Temple 148
Ezra 149

Nehemiah

Nehemiah 153
Nehemiah Teaches the Law...................................... 154

Esther

Queen Vashti... 157
Queen Esther 158
Queen Esther's Plight 159
Haman 160
The End of Haman.. 162

Job

Job 165
Job—An Upright Man... 167
Satan Attacks.. 168
Job's Death.. 169

Psalms

Psalms.. 173
I Will Bless the Lord 174
Praise the Lord 175
Praise Him Forever.. 176

Proverbs

Wisdom and Instruction 179

God Hates.. 180

The Harlot's House 181

Receive Wisdom's Instruction... 182

Wisdom 183

Still More Wisdom.. 184

Who Can Find a Faithful Man?.. 185

Who Can Find a Virtuous Wife.. 186

Ecclesiastes

A Wise King Falls 189

There's a Time 190

Vanity... 191

Death Comes to Good and Bad.. 192

Song of Solomon

Black, But Comely... 195

Song of Solomon 196

Isaiah

The Day of the Lord of Host... 199

Woe to Strong Drink... 200

Look Forward 201

The Fall of Lucifer 202

Woe to Those Not Trusting Him.. 203

Lift Up Your Eyes on High 204

No Other God.. 205

The Prophecy of Christ... 206

Daughters of Zion 207

Jeremiah

Jeremiah, the Prophet.. 211
Hear God's Word 213
Hananiah 214
Nothing is too Hard 215

Lamentations

God was Angry 219
I Called Upon Thy Name.. 220
Restore Us, Lord... 221

Ezekiel

Ezekiel's Vision.. 225
Israel's Message 227
Dry Bones 228

Daniel

For God is My Judge 231
The King's Golden Image... 233
A Second Dream 234
The Writing on the Wall.. 235
Daniel 236
Daniel's Dream... 237

Hosea

Hosea's Family.. 241
Hosea's Unfaithful Wife.. 242
Israel—The Harlot 243
Come Home, Backslider 244

Joel

Joel—The Prophet 247
God's Wonders 248
The Day of the Lord 250

Amos

Amos 253
Hear Ye this Word 254
Amos Prophesied 255

Obadiah

The Vision of Obadiah 259

Jonah

Jonah's Lesson 263

Micah

The Wicked Rules 267
The Joy of Restoration 268
Woe is Me! 269

Nahum

Nahum's Vision 273

Habakkuk

The Chaldean's Rule 277
Habakkuk's Prayer 279

Zephaniah

Zephaniah's Warning 283
God is in the Midst 284

Haggai

It is Time The Book of Haggai.................................... 287
Haggai Speaks Again 288

Zechariah

Thus Said the Lord of Host 291
When Zechariah Asked 293

Malachi

Malachi 297
Will Man Rob God 298

NEW TESTAMENT

Mathew

Matthew... 303
Jesus was Born 304
The Nazarene 305
The Temptation of Jesus 306
The Beatitudes 307
Be Blessed His Twelve.. 309
A Sea Walk... 310
He Arose 311

Mark

Following Jesus... 315
I'm Sure He's the One 316
The Death of John, the Baptist.................................. 317
He Does All Things Well 318
The Signs? 319
Go Ye Into All the World.. 320

Luke

Jesus at Twelve 323
Preaching in the Wilderness 324
Rebuking Devils and Diseases 325
Follow Me 326
The Alabaster Box 327
The Prodigal Son 328
The Lost is Found 329
Saying Good-bye 330

John

The Samaritans Believed 333
The Day of the Feast 334
The First Stone 335
Verily, Verily 336
Jesus Wept 337
The Good Shepherd 338
The Last Supper 339
Jesus Prays 340
His Time Has Come 341
The Cock Crew 342
It is Finished 343

The Acts

The Almighty Holy Ghost 347
Lies and Death 348
Acts of the Apostles 349
Paul and Barnabas Depart 351

Romans

The Book of Romans 355

Going Against Nature 356
Judge Not 357
Justified by Faith 358
God Forbid 359
The Wages of Sin is Death 360
A Thankful Day 361

1 Corinthians

To the Church 365
Labor Together 366
Sexual Sin 367
Better to Marry 368
Run the Race 369
Be Worthy 370
Charity 371
We Shall Live Again 372

2 Corinthians

2 Corinthians By Faith not Sight 375
Giving to God 376

Galatians

Galatians 379
Live in the Spirit 380

Ephesians

The Epistle of Paul to the Ephesians 383
Good Works 384
Walk in the Light 385
Christ is the Head 386

Philippians

The Epistle of Paul to the Philippians 389

Run Not in Vain.. 390

God Supplies Our Needs 391

Colossians

The Epistle of Paul to the Colossians.................................... 395

1 Thessalonians

The First Epistle of Paul to the Thessalonians 399

Good Advice 400

Watch and Be Sober.. 401

Grace Be with You 402

2 Thessalonians

The Second Epistle of Paul to the Thessalonians 405

Concerning the Coming 406

1 Timothy

The First Epistle of Paul to Timothy...................................... 409

Pray for All Men 410

2 Timothy

Timothy's Second Letter... 413

Depart from Inquity.. 414

Know This... 415

Titus

The Epistle of Paul to Titus 419

Elders 420

Philemon

The Epistle of Paul to Philemon 423

Hebrews

Hebrews... 427
Crowned with Glory... 428
The Same Mouth.. 429
Fervent Prayers Avails Much 430
If God Permits... 431
Have Faith... 432
The Same God Forever... 434

James

James.. 437
A Deadly Tongue.. 438
Resist the World... 439
Being Patient... 440

1 Peter

The First Epistle of Peter 443
Flesh is Like Grass... 444
Do Good Not Evil... 445

2 Peter

The Lack of Knowledge 449
The Lord Knows... 450

1 John

The First Epistle of John The Truth is the Light....................... 453
We Have an Advocate 454

Love Not the World.. 455
Believe Not Every Spirit 456
Whosoever Believes 457

2 John

The Second Epistle of John For the Truth's Sake.................... 461

3 John

The Third Epistle of John Greet Friends by Name................... 465

Jude

Jude 469

Revelation

The Revelation of John The Devine Introduction.................... 473
Alpha and Omega, the Almighty 474
He Reveled to John.. 475

GENESIS

The Beginning

I heard today they just discovered
two new planets in our universe.
In the beginning God created
all the heavens and the earth.

He hung the stars so bright,
and isn't it wonderful how
He makes them shine at night?
He only had to say "Let there be light."

He hung the Sun
in just the right place,
to keep us warm, give us light, but
not too close to burn up the human race.

Man is constantly discovering how
wonderful God is to him.
We should always want to give
the highest praise to Him.

"Let there be light"
separated night from day.
He made the earth so we could live,
but to live in God's way.

He made the universe, but
the best was yet to come.
The miracles of man and beast
let God's will be done.

And God saw all that he made and it was good
(Gen. 1:31)

Adam and Eve

God formed the first man from
the dust; Adam was his name.
He was created in the image of God.
Over creation man did reign.

God gave him dominion over
the sea, the land, and the air.
God didn't want Adam to be alone,
so He also put woman there.

Although Adam came from earth's
dust, woman came from his side,
to live in a garden of Eden,
a perfect place for them to abide.

Until one day the serpent raised
up his ugly head;
he caused Eve to tempt Adam,
then their perfect life was dead.

Adam was cursed to toil for food,
Eve to bear children in pain.
Don't listen to the devil, children,
because deceiving you is his aim.

Eve Listened

Eve listened to the snake;
she ate of the fruit,
knowing full well that
God told them what not to do.

God told her and Adam,
"If you eat it you will surely die,
for this tree of knowledge
will open up your eye."

But Eve listened to the snake;
she ate and gave Adam some too.
He took a big bite; good
and evil they then knew.

They both became aware that
they did not have on clothes.
They gathered up some leaves
so their nakedness did not show.

What a price to pay;
sin was no longer dead.
Eve, you silly woman,
you put evil into our heads.

Cain and Abel

Eve bore two sons;
Cain and Abel were their names—
two different personalities,
certainly not the same.

One was a sheep keeper,
the other toiled the ground,
until it came to pass,
Cain didn't want Abel around.

You see, they both brought God
an offering, one of fruit, the other fat.
God respected Abel's offering,
and He turned Cain's back.

Cain got so angry—yes, that man was mad—
in his angry state, he did something bad.

He killed his brother
while they were in the field.
Wrong move, my brother;
that was certainly not God's will.

"Am I my brother's keeper?" he
answered when God asked where he was at.
Wrong answer, brother Cain;
God already know that fact.

God then cursed him;
he became a vagabond.
Vengeance is the Lord's, my friend;
and He will get it done.

Methuselah

It's hard to imagine living
so many, many years,
like the men before the flood—
over nine hundred, don't you hear?

Methuselah, who was the oldest,
was nine hundred sixty-nine.
And people call you old at sixty
in this day and time.

We celebrate each year we have
at our birthday parties,
trying not to tell our age
after we turn forty.

What good is longevity, if you
do nothing with that life;
if you spend all those years
living long, without Christ?

Noah

Here's a story about Noah, who was really smart.
God chose him to build the ark.
"The rain will come. You'd better get ready.
It's going to rain, and it will get heavy.

"Take the animals on board, two by two.
And go aboard and take your family with you."
When you finish, God will lock the door.
"Sorry, sinner, can't take no more."

It rained forty days, and it rained forty nights.
The water rose up, with no land in sight.
He sent forth a dove; when it stayed away,
he knew it was drying and they could leave some day.

"Go forth, you sons, take your wives with you,
and all the animals, two by two.

"Go be fruitful. Breed and give birth.
Then you will multiply on this earth."

The Rainbow

"I shall send you a sign—one never seen before—
something you will see after every downpour.

"A rainbow you shall call it,
of yellow, blue, and green,
shining through the clouds.
It's beauty you've never seen.

"It will be a covenant
I will make to you this day—
Earth will never be destroyed by flood,
never again this way."

Remember God's covenant to all flesh,
because this is true—
He gave His word to Noah,
and it's also meant for you.

Noah lived after the flood 950 years; and he died
(Gen. 9:29).

Babel

The whole world was one language;
we could all understand each other.
That gave them an idea—
one that makes you say "O brother."

You see, they would build a tower;
to reach heaven was their endeavor.
To call on God uninvited, well,
they thought that very clever.

But God came down to see them—
their tower and their city.
He began to change things,
and He showed them no pity.

He scattered them abroad,
and He changed their speech.
They no longer understood each other;
that threw them off their feet.

The city was known as Babel,
because the Lord had His way.
We were given different languages,
which we still have today.

(Gen. 11)

Abram and Lot

Terah begot Abram and Haran.
Haran begot Abram's nephew, Lot.
Abram's wife was Sarai, whom he loved,
but children they had not.

Terah took Lot, Abram, and Sarai
from Ur to the Canaan land.
They stopped in Harah, where they lived
until Terah died, being a blessed man.

Now the Lord said to Abram,
"Get out, it's time to go
to a land I will show you,
where I will bless you so.

"I will bless those that bless you,
and curse back those who do not.
Take Sarai, your wife, with you,
also your nephew, Lot."

When Abram began this journey
at the age of seventy-five,
now even at this age,
Sarai was a beautiful wife.

Abram and Sarai

Abram told Sarai, "When we get there,
pretend you are not my wife.
A woman of your beauty
could cause the men to take my life.

"Just tell them when they ask you,
you are indeed my sister, dear.
We can pass through their land
without you shedding a single tear."

But Pharaoh found favor
in her beauty, which was fair.
He paid Abram lots of kindness
so he could keep her there.

But God did not approve
of Abram's silly plan.
He sent plagues on Pharaoh's house;
Pharaoh then sent them from his land.

"Why didn't you just tell us that
this beauty was your wife?
You could have told the truth.
You didn't have to hide."

(God's name change for Abram and
Sarai was Abraham and Sarah)
(Gen 7:5,15)

Lot

Two angels came to Sodom, as Lot sat at the gate.
Lot rose to meet them; he invited them in his home to stay.
He said, "Tarry here the night. Rest and wash your feet."
They said, "Nay, we will abide here. We'll sleep in the street."

Lot begged them, and they did come in to sleep and to eat.
Lot then had his servant to prepare them such a feast.
Before they could lay down to sleep, the
men of Sodom came around.
They called to Lot, "Where are the men we heard are in town?"

Lot called out, "Go away. Take your wickedness away from here.
I will give you my virgin daughters, this I do swear."
When the men said no, and tried to enter into Lot's house,
they were then struck blind, right then, every louse.

The angels then told Lot, "Take your family from this evil place,
for it shall be destroyed soon—it shall become a waste."
Lot, his wife, and daughters were told
to go. "But look not behind,
for this is God's will, and His will be thou thine."

As the fire and the brimstone landed on these towns,
Lot's wife must have forgotten, for she turned to look around.
When she did, she was turned into a pillar of salt.
But God remembered Abraham, Lot's soul was not lost.

Read of Lot, and Sodom and Gomorrah
(Gen. 19:1-38).

Father Abraham

An angel cried from heaven.
Abraham answered, "Here am I."
"God has sent the message—
your son Isaac will not die."

An angel called Abraham,
called him a second time,
"The Lord has blessed your seed,
and like the stars thy seed shall shine."

Abraham was old, and he was
blessed in all things.
Trust the Lord, saints,
He only says what He means.

Sarah, Abraham's wife, was
one hundred twenty-seven when she died.
Abraham lived on
to see Isaac take a bride.

Now don't you want God on your side?

Then again Abraham took a wife.
Her name was Keturah
(Gen. 25:1)

Then Abraham gave up the ghost and died...
(Gen. 25:8)

Abraham's Seed

God told Abram, "You shall now be Abraham,
and you and I will make a deal.
Just trust in Me, your Father,
and you must do My will.

"Although you're old and you're
way past your prime,
you will be the father of nations
as long as your will is Mine.

"Sarai, now Sarah, shall bear him—
Isaac will be his name.
I will bless your seed forever—
from him prince and kings shall reign.

"Ishmael, Isaac, and others, all
fathered by you, Abraham,
as your father, God, has promised,
you can trust the Great I Am."

As for Me, behold my covenant is with thee,
and thou shall be a father of many nations (....)

Isaac's Wife

Isaac went on a journey to his kindred,
there to take a wife.
Abraham did not want
just anyone in his life.

He met a lovely damsel,
whose family took him in.
The Lord, of course, had guided him
to his father's brethren.

He said to her father,
"My father has sent me here,
to take a wife from my kindred—
He made that loud and clear.

"I asked her for some water,
and she drew some for me.
I would like to marry her,
if it would please thee."

Her father said to Isaac's servants,
"Take Rebecca and go.
This is the will of God,
and I know he loves her so."

(Gen. 24)

Ishmael

After Isaac was born to Sarah who
was old, and she gave suck,
Abraham's firstborn son by Hagar
mocked her, and she made quite a fuss.

She told Abraham to cast this
bondwoman and her son out.
"We must get rid of them right now,
so our son's inheritance is without doubt."

It grieved Abraham's heart to have
to tell his firstborn son to go.
God said it was alright. "He is
blessed, I Am has said so."

Hagar took Ishmael and wandered in
the wilderness until the water was gone.
She thought we will surely die out
Here, for we have no home.

But God provided a well, and Ishmael
grew and became a great nation too.
When God makes a promise, He
will always do as He said He will do.

(Gen. 21)

Jacob and Esau

Abraham's sons Isaac and Ishmael buried him in a cave
(Gen. 25:9)

Now Isaac had a problem,
and this is what it was—
his older brother had lots of children,
but he got none from his love.

Finally Rebecca conceived and gave birth to twins—
twins that fought each other as they were still within.
The Lord spoke unto her, said, "You have
two nations in thy womb.
The older shall serve the younger, born to you real soon."

The firstborn was Esau—
all red and full of hair.
Jacob came out holding on to his brother's heel,
as if he was saying "You cannot leave me there."

Now Esau was a hunter, who cooked his kill for his dad.
Jacob stayed in the tent; his mother's love he had.
Isaac gave to Jacob Esau's birthright, for
he was old and could not see.
The old shall serve the youngest one is how it had to be.

And the Lord said unto her two nations are in thy womb....
.... the elder shall serve the younger
(Gen. 25:9)

Jacob's Ladder

Isaac blessed Jacob and sent him away to take a wife,
so he could be fruitful and his seed could multiply.
As Jacob journeyed, he was tired,
and settled down for the night.
He dreamed of a ladder ascending into heaven—
Lord, it was quite a sight.

The ladder that he dreamed o
reached into heaven, and behold,
angels of God came up and down it,
is what I have been told.

God Himself came to him—
the God of Abraham, Isaac, and Jacob.
He told him how he'd bless him—
how his seed would fill this world up.

Jacob awoke out of his sleep
with fear in his heart.
Surely God had visited him,
so he would leave a mark.

He marked it, and he named it,
then he made a vow—
"If God will be with me,
I'll serve Him here right now."

(Gen. 28:12)

Jacob Wrestled God

One night in Jacob's travels with his
two wives, their servants, and eleven sons,
he sent them ahead of him,
so he could be just one.

That night a man wrestled him
until the breaking day.
He touched the socket of his hip;
it made him walk a different way.

He asked Jacob to let him go,
for the day breaks.
"Not until you bless me,
right now, for heaven's sake."

"What is your name?" he asked,
and Jacob answered him.
"Your name shall now be Israel,
not Jacob, not Jake, or Jim."

Israel said, "I have seen God
face to face, and I am yet alive.
I make this promise, here and now,
I'll never leave His side.

"From this day forth, although
I shall always walk with a limp,
I will no longer eat the shank
that comes from the hip."

But Esau ran to meet him and embraced him and
fell on his neck, and kissed him, and they wept
(Gen.33:4)

Jacob's Wives

Jacob's story of his wife was
somewhat like his father's.
He also went to the land of his kindred
to marry someone's daughter.

Soon he came to a well where
there were sheep all around.
The well had a stone covering it,
so they couldn't let the bucket down.

Jacob saw a girl coming
to the well with her sheep.
He knew when he saw this girl
that she was the one to keep.

He agreed to work for Rachel,
so he worked seven years.
But he was given her older sister
to keep him working here.

So Isaac worked for Rachel.
He worked seven years more.
He took both his wives with him,
and he was out the door.

Leah, Jacob's first wife, bore him seven sons.
Rachel, his true, true love,
well, she just couldn't have none.

But God remembered Rachel;
she conceived and bore a son.
The Lord truly blessed her,
and he was not the only one.

Joseph and Benjamin found favor in their father's eye.

Joseph

Joseph, as a little boy, without
a doubt his father's favorite—
he ran around doing this and that
while his older brothers labored.

His father made him a coat,
and it had many, many colors.
He would run around and flaunt it
before his jealous older brothers.

Then he started having dreams
that made him above the rest.
His brothers really got mad;
they thought killing him would be best.

Brother Rueben saved his life that day,
and they threw him in a hole.
"I cannot kill my brother," said he,
if the truth be told.

They sold Joseph to a caravan,
and told his father he was dead.
Don't feel sorry for Joseph, though;
his destiny lies ahead.

(Gen. 37)

Joseph, the Slave

Joseph was taken into Egypt.
He found favor in his master's eye.
Just because bad things happen,
don't give up the ghost and die.

He was all grown-up, and
was now a handsome man.
His mistress tried to lay with him;
he ran leaving his garment in her hand.

Joseph's master put him in prison.
He again found favor in their sights.
Even when things went bad,
he was never far from his God's might.

While in prison, Pharaoh's butler and baker,
both of them had dreams.
They could not figure them out
because nothing was as it seemed.

They told their dreams to Joseph.
What he interpreted sure came true.
"The butler will live and leave this place,
but the news is bad for you."

Pharaoh hung the chief baker.
The chief butler was restored just like that.
The chief butler forgot Joseph
as soon as he turned his back.

(Gen. 40)

Topman

Behold it came to pass, after two full years, Pharaoh had a dream
(Gen. 41)

Pharaoh said to Joseph, "Behold, I've had a dream.
And no one can interpret it.
I've asked everyone I know,
but no one can do it yet.

"My chief butler told me
that you have done this before.
To understand these dreams
I would open every door."

Joseph told Pharaoh, "Seven years
good grain will come to you.
The famine comes for seven years.
Now I'll tell you what to do.

"You must gather all the grain,
store it every day,
so when the famine comes,
it won't hurt you in any way."

Pharaoh believed Joseph;
made him his topman.
He was to be obeyed—
that was Pharaoh's command.

*And Pharaoh said unto Joseph, see I have
set thee over all the land of Egypt*
(Gen. 41:41)

A Family Reunited

But as for you, you meant evil against
me, but God meant it for good....
(Gen. 50:20)

We've all heard the story of how bad was turned to good.
Joseph, sold by his brothers,
was now ruler of the people, like his dreams said he would.

Lo and behold, the famine hit Israel too.
They had to go to Egypt, that's all that they could do.

They went to see the ruler, not knowing it was he,
to buy grain from Egypt to feed their family.

Joseph looked so different, his brothers did not recognize him.
Joseph, of course, knew at once, for he could not forget them.

He found out first of all, if his father was alive.
Then he plotted how he could get his
younger brother by his side.

He played a trick or two, until he could wait no more.
"Hey, brothers, it's me—Joseph, and I'm not even sore."

So they cried together, hugs and kisses too.
"I just can't tell you how much I've missed you."

So they gathered up their father; and the family, one and all,
came to live in Egypt; it was the beginning of Israel's fall.

I love to read this story; it brings out my tears.
They finally are united after all those years.

*All these are the twelve tribes of Israel and this is what
their father spoke to them. And he blessed them....*
(Gen. 49:28)

The Twelve Tribes

"Gather and hear, you sons of Jacob.
Listen to what your father has to say.

"**Rueben**, the firstborn, the beginning of my
strength, until you defiled it one day.

"**Simeon** and **Levi,** you are brothers
who run a cruel dwelling place,
cursed be your anger and wrath
that can only lead to waste.

"**Judah,** whom your brothers praise,
lies down as does a lion.
His lips white with milk, and
eyes darkened with wine.

"**Zebulun** shall dwell by the haven of the sea.
While **Issachar,** lying between two burdens, is strong as can be.
Dan shall judge his people, as one of the Israel tribes,
a serpent by the path, and a viper by the wayside.

"**Gad,** a troop shall trample upon him,
but he shall overcome at last.
Out of **Asher** shall his bread be fat.
He shall yield royal dainties with class.

"**Niphtali** is a hind let loose.
He giveth goodly word.
Joseph is a fruitful bough, who has been hated,
but now he is heard.

"**Benjamin,** my youngest, shall be ravenous
as a wolf eating his prey.
In the morning he shall eat.
At night he'll give it away.

"All these are the twelve tribes of Israel.
I, their father, have spoken to them.
I will bless you as I leave you,
for my life groweth real dim."

*And when Jacob had made an end of
commanding his sons, he gathered up his feet
into the bed and yielded up the ghost...*
(Gen. 49:33)

So Joseph died being one hundred ten years old...
(Gen. 50:26)

EXODUS

A New Generatio
(Exodus)

Joseph, his brothers, and
all their generation died.
But the children of Israel
grew fruitful and multiplied.

The new king of Egypt said, "Look, the people
of Israel are more and mightier than we.
Let's deal shrewdly with them
before they join our enemies."

So they set them task and burdens.
Well, they made them slaves.
They worked the Israelite children
right into the grave.

The Israelites multiplied;
they became more and more,
until the king decreed
to kill all male babies borne.

The midwives feared God,
and they could not do this thing.
They did not kill the male children,
which did not please the king.

And Pharaoh charged all his people saying;
every son that is born ye shall cast into the river,
and every daughter ye shall save alive
(Exodus 1:22)

Baby Moses

A Levi woman conceived
and bore a goodly son.
She hid him three months, but
something had to be done.

She made a small ark of

bulrushes, slime, and pitch;
placed her male child in it;
then she placed it in the ditch.

Her daughter watched him travel
down the riverside,
where Pharaoh's daughter found
Him; she kept him alive.

Although his real mother nursed him,
he came to be Pharaoh's daughter's son.
She called his name Moses,
long before he had to run.

One day Moses, while among his brethren,
saw an Egyptian smite a Hebrew.
Moses killed the Egyptian,
because his anger began to brew.

So Moses ran away, to keep
Pharaoh from killing him.
He dwelled in a place called Midian.
Now the Hebrews' lives looked dim.

(Exod. 2)

The Burning Bush

Moses came to live in a foreign land.
He married Zipporah; had a son; was a happy man.
While back in Egypt, there arose a new king,
to the children of Israel, this didn't mean a thing.

They cried out to the Lord in bondage,
and He heard their cry.
"We call upon the God of Abraham.
Lord hear us and tell us why."

Meanwhile Moses was attending the flock
of Jethro, his father-in-law.
He came to the mountain of God;
something was burning—this is what he saw.

There in the distance, a bush was burning,
but fire consumed it not.
He turned aside to see it burn
with God in it; I know it was hot.

He heard a voice from within
call him, and he answered, "Here am I."
"Take off your shoes on holy ground,
then I shall tell you why.

"I, the God of Abraham, have
a job for you to do.
You must lead my people out of bondage.
I know I can count on you."

(Exodus 3)

And God said unto Moses, I AM, THAT I AM
(Ex. 3:14)

Moses

I Am told Moses to set His people free.
"Go down into Egypt—that's where they will be.
Go and tell Pharaoh it's time to give them up.
Don't be afraid to tell him, he'd just better duck.

"Go and take Aaron, and I will have your back.
My signs and My wonders will
show the Egyptians just where I am at.

"Water will become blood, then frogs, lice, and flies,
then diseases, boils, and locusts, until his first son dies.

"Lead My children, Moses, through the Red Sea.
And on the land
milk and honey awaits you,
every woman, child, and man.

"Come up into the mountains.
Come, Moses, you and I.
I will give you Ten Commandments—
laws to live by."

(Exodus)

Pharoah's End

"Lift up thy rod, Moses, and
stretch out thine hand
over the sea and divide it. Let
the children of Israel pass over
and walk on dry land.

"I shall harden the hearts of the Egyptians,
and they shall try to follow you.
Pharaoh and all his chariots
will not make it through.

"Then the Egyptians will know that
I am the Lord God for sure,
as the sea closes upon them
and only My people shall endure."

Then Israel saw the great work
upon the Egyptians that the Lord did.
They then feared the Lord and believed.
They then feared Moses and did what he bid.

(Exod. 14)

Have You Heard the Story?

Have you heard the story of how
Moses, with his staff in his hand,
led the Hebrew children through the Red Sea,
and they crossed on dry land?

And of how Pharaoh's army,
well, they tried to do the same,
but the waters of the Red Sea
caught them as they came?

Now the Hebrew children found fault.
They complained of this and that.
Even after so many miracles,
they talked of going back.

Aaron, Moses's brother, he too
did some very bad things.
He made a golden calf to worship,
out of their gold necklaces and rings.

God gave to Moses Ten Commandments—
rules by which to live.
Thank you, Heavenly Father,
for the love you give and give.

The Amalek War

Hold up the rod of God real high,
so His people will prevail and stand tall.
When your arms fall down, the Amalekites win
and the Israelites army will stall.

But Moses's hands were heavy,
and he grew tired of standing too.
They placed a stone under him, and said, "Aaron
and Hur will help you."

They held his arms up for him,
each one on either side,
until the sun went down, victory
went to God's people—the Israelites.

The Lord told Moses to write this
for a memorial in a book—
"This war will continue from generation
to generation, for this is what it took.

"Because of God's covenant with you,
and the people's doubt,
this war will go on for generations,
until God Himself puts it out."

(Exod. 17)

God's Mercy Seat

(Exod. 25:22)

My Heavenly Father met Moses
above the mercy seat.
From between the two cherubim on the ark,
from there He did speak.

He gives us new mercies,
and He gives them everyday.
Come sit on the seat of mercy,
and hear what He has to say.

The Lord has mercy on us sinners;
He gives it every time.
Just ask, and you will receive it;
His mercy will be thine.

To sit on the mercy seat, my
sins could wear it out.
My Lord forgave me of those sins,
of that I have no doubt.

Sinners, won't you come and sit;
this seat is for you too.
Come, receive His mercy;
see what He'll do for you.

You shall make a mercy seat of pure gold; two and a half
cubits shall it length and a cubit and a half it's width
(Exod. 25:17)

LEVITICUS

Sacrifices Unto God

Leviticus

The third book of Moses,
called Leviticus by name,
tells us how God wanted His sacrifices
and how to do His offerings.

He said to bring your cattle and your sheep—
a male without blemish at all.
Cut them up and burn them—
a sweet aroma unto God.

The offering must be perfect,
for God don't accept no junk.
Don't bring Him any blemishes,
nor don't bring Him a runt.

An offering of fine flour shall be
an offering for the meal.
Pour oil and frankincense upon it;
a sweet aroma it shall yield.

A peace offering shall also be offered,
of male or female from the flock.
These offerings must be the best—
only the best of what you've got.

... an offering made by fire, of a sweet savor unto the Lord
(Lev. 1:13)

Eating Holy Things

And the Lord spoke unto Moses and Aaron,
saying unto them thus—
"Speak unto the children of Israel to
hear this, for this is a must.

"These are the beast among the beast on
the earth that you can eat,
whichever chews the cud, and is cloven-
footed and parted-hoofed is your meat.

"Not a camel, because a camel is unclean,
not the coney or the hare,
nor the swine, you shall eat.
Choose your meat with care.

"These you shall eat of the waters—
all those whichever have scales or fins
in the seas and rivers you shall eat—
if no scales or fins, you will leave them in.

"Among the fowls, no don't eat raven, owl,
or hawk, the stork, heron, or bat,
but eat of the locust, beetle, and grasshopper,
and such kinds as that."

All flying insects that creep on all fours
shall be an abomination to you
(Lev. 11:20)

(Lev. 11)

I Am Your God

"You shall not make unto you idols or
graven images, or set up images of stone,
or bow down to them, as I am God—
I am your God alone.

"You shall keep my Sabbaths and revere
My sanctuary and walk in My laws.
You shall keep my commandments and
live them—you must live them all.

"Then I will give rain in due season,
and I will give peace in the land.
You shall lie down and not be afraid—
I will keep you safe in My hands.

"Five of you shall chase a hundred, and
a hundred will put ten thousand to flight.
Your enemies shall fall before you by the
Sword, and I will keep you in My sights."

(Lev. 26)

*And I will walk among you, and will be
your God, and ye shall be My people*
(Lev. 26:12)

NUMBERS

Numbers

The Lord spoke to Moses in the wilderness,
in the tabernacle where they met;
told him to take a census of all
the people, so he could see where he was at.

God called out names of leaders;
Moses and Aaron took those he named.
They counted all the tribes of Israel;
separated the warriors to be trained.

He separated the clean from the unclean;
told him how to deal with an unfaithful wife.
He separated the Levites from among them;
their dedication had to be just right.

The Lord met with Moses again
above the mercy seat.
Between the cherubim on the ark,
again the Lord did speak.

Milk and Honey Land

And the Lord told Moses to send out
men to search the Canaan land.
"The land I gave to the Israelites' children.
From the tribes send each a man."

So they went out and came to Eshcol,
where they cut a cluster of grapes.
It took two to bare it, also
pomegranates and figs heavy in weight.

After forty days, they returned
to show the people the fruit they ate.
It flowed with milk and honey all right,
but the people there were great.

The people cried all night; they wept
and wished they had stayed in Egypt to die.
"God brought us to this wilderness,"
they complained and asked God why.

Now God don't like complainers,
so He just punished them,
"Your carcasses will fall here.
Forty years your children will wander 'cause
you do not question Him."

(Num. 14)

DEUTERONOMY

The Defeat of Og

... that Moses spake unto the children of Israel...
(Deut. 1:3)

Og, the king of Bashan, came out against us—
he and all of his people into battle.
The Lord said, "Fear him not, for He will deliver
him, his land, his people, and his cattle."

We smote Og and all his people,
until none was left of him.
We took all his cities in the kingdom—
a great many; we took all of them.

The Lord your God has given you this
land to possess it and to abide.
Your cattle and your little ones
shall live there with your wives.

I command Joshua saying "Your eyes
have seen all the Lord has done.
The Lord will fight for you.
Remember this—His work has just begun."

So we abode in the valley over against Beth-peor
(Deut. 3:29)

Ten Commandments

And Moses called all of Israel unto him.
"Hear, O Israel, the judgments and the laws,
that you may learn and keep them,
and live them one and all.

"The Lord made this covenant with us,
and not our fathers, but us.
He has brought us out of bondage.
Listen, His Word is thus:

"I am the Lord thy God. There shall be
none other gods before me,
no graven images, or any likenesses
of anything shall there be.

"You shall not take the name of your God
in vain. Keep the Sabbath day holy—
six days shall you and your household
work—on the Sabbath, no work totally.

"Honor thy father and thy mother as
God has commanded you. Do not kill,
neither shall you commit adultery,
neither shall you steal.

"Neither shall you bear false witness
against your neighbor—do not lie.
You shall not covet thy neighbor's house
or field, or desire your neighbor's wife."

(Deut. 5:1-21)

These words the Lord spake unto all your assembly...
(Deut. 5:22)

Fear the Lord

"Fear the Lord thy God, to keep all His
statutes, which I command you and your sons,
all the days of your life, that
your days may be prolonged.

"Hear therefore, O Israel, and observe it
that you may increase mightily,
as the Lord God has promised a land
that flows with milk and honey.

"The Lord our God is one Lord, and we
shall love Him with all our hearts and might.
Teach these words to your children—let
them be as frontlets in their sights.

"Write them on the post of your house,
and write them on your gates.
Carry them with you into the land
of honey and milk and dates."

(Deut. 6:1-8)

JOSHUA

Joshua

God spoke to Joshua, son of Nun,
saying, "Moses, my servant, is dead.
Now, therefore arise, go into Jordan,
for you are now the Israelites head.

"No man will be able to stand before you
all the days of your life.
I will not leave you or forsake you
as long as you live life right.

"Be strong and very courageous, that
you may do according to all the law.
Night and day you may observe,
to tell others what you have saw."

Joshua commanded the officers saying,
"Prepare to cross over Jordan. We leave
in three days.
God has given us this land to possess it,
and I must believe what He says and in His ways."

They answered saying "We have heeded
Moses in all things. Now we will heed you.
Whosoever rebels and do not listen
will die, for rebellion will not do."

Cross Over Jordan

God told Joshua to cross the Jordan River
when it was overflowing its banks.
Joshua believed in God's works, so
he gave Him his praise, not his can'ts.

God said, "Tell the priest to cross over
with the Ark of the Lord."
When they stepped into the water,
well, the water began to part.

Joshua took twelve men—
one man for each of the tribes.
To enter the dry place in the Jordan, he
told each to get a stone from inside.

After the priest and the people
crossed over, it came to pass—
God commanded the water to flow again; the
banks flowed again—they flowed real fast.

They placed the twelve stones in Gilgal,
so that all the people could see
a memorial of stones to God,
and for the people some history.

Remember where God has a hand,
you will always cross on dry land.

For the Lord your God dried up the waters of Jordan
from before you until ye were passed over...
(Josh. 4:23)

Rahab

Joshua sent two men into Jericho
to go view the land.
They came to a harlot named Rahab's house,
and she gave them a hand.

When the King came looking for them,
she told the men to hide;
she told the King they had gone from there,
knowing they were still inside.

The pursuers left; she came and got them,
and said, "Before you go,
I know your God is the only God,
who gave you this land, I know.

"So please spare us, my father's household;
please spare my kin.
Just give me a true token that
will spare us as your army comes in."

They said unto her as
she gave them a scarlet rope,
"Hang this rope, so we can see it.
You will be spared from the smote."

Then Joshua spared Rahab the harlot,
her father's household, and all that she had...
(Josh. 6:25)

The Walls Fell

God again told Joshua how to take
the city of Jericho, and it came to pass—
the Israelites could get ready
to see the promised land at last.

Although there were walls
with the king and his men inside,
they thought themselves safe
with a good place to stay alive.

Now God told Joshua how to breach
the walls, and they would come down.
"Do as I tell you to do,
and you will own this town."

So seven priests bearing ram horns,
before the Ark they blew.
They compassed the city once—
that was on day two.

Each day of blowing and returning to
Camp, for six days they did this.
On the seventh day they went out,
but there was a different twist.

The seventh day, they compassed
the city seven times that day.
The seventh day, the people shouted,
the walls fell, and the Israelites had their way.

They spared Rahab's household;
everything else belonged to them.
The Lord was with Joshua,
but all praises belong to Him.

Secret Sin

The Lord woke Joshua one morning saying,
"Why do you lie on your face?
There is sin among you—
someone has caused you disgrace.

"Not only have they stole stuff, but
they are trying to hide.
If you do not find this person,
I will leave your side."

Joshua brought the tribes before him.
He searched for the "secret sin."
Although Achan had buried his spoils,
God knows the heart of all men.

Joshua called the people to sanctification,
because of the sin Achan did.
One sin thought by he to be secret;
he sure thought it was hid.

If you think you have gotten away
with a sin kept deep inside you.
There is no secret from God, my friend,
for God knows all that we do.

(Josh. 7)

Joshua's Death

The land was captured by Joshua,
then divided among the tribes,
from border to border in the land
to the Jordan toward the sunrise.

They gave the city he asked for
to Joshua, the son of Nun,
according to the Word of the Lord,
for a job well done.

The Lord gave to Israel all the land
He had sworn to their fathers.
They took possession and lived there,
while their enemies faltered.

Now it came to pass that
Joshua, the son of Nun, died.
Being one hundred and ten years old,
Joshua died on the Lord's side.

(Josh. 24:29)

JUDGES

Judges

God sent an angel to bring
Israel this news—
"You have not driven out the inhabitants,
in fact you're being used.

"You didn't tear down their altars
or drive the inhabitants out.
Now you shall suffer,
of that have no doubt.

"They and their gods shall be
a thorn in your sides."
After the angel spoke,
the people of Israel cried.

There arose a new generation
after Joshua died,
who did not know the Lord,
and did evil in His sight.

The Lord was against them,
and they became distressed.
So he sent them judges
to get them out that mess.

Still they would not listen;
still they followed other gods;
still a hardheaded people,
they were just plain odd.

Then God got angry and
sold them into the king's hands.
There was then forty years' rest
in the land.

... and the children of Israel did evil
again in the sight of the Lord...
(Judg. 3:12)

God's Women

Now Deborah was a model for any woman.
She let the Spirit of God shape her life.
She was a prophetess judging Israel.
She was also Lapidoth's wife.

She made decisions for her people,
and she was a military advisor.
She had insight into warfare,
for she had the Lord to guide her.

Then there was Jael, the wife of Heber.
She invited Sisera into her tent.
She gave him food, drink, and blankets.
He died, not knowing what all that meant.

So let all thine enemies perish, O Lord...
And the land had rest forty years
Judg. 5:31)

Gideon

It seems like every few years,
Israel did evil in God's sight
like the people of today;
we just can't get it right.

God keeps forgiving us over and over again.
We repent for a while, then go right back to sin.

God sent an angel to Gideon
as he threshed wheat in a field.
"Come, God is calling you.
It's time to do His will."

Gideon answered saying, "I am least in my father's house.
Surely, not me, I certainly have no clout."

"Gideon, you are a mighty man of valor.
You have found favor in my sight today.
Go destroy Baal's altars.
I will show you My way."

Gideon tested God by placing a fleece
of dry wool on the threshing floor.
The next morning he squeezed out water
about a cup or more.

He tested God again, and did it the other way;
the fleece was completely dry,
but the ground was wet that day.

Why are we always testing?
Can't we obey as God said we should?
It seems we are always
knocking our hardheads on wood.

Now Gideon died at a good old age...
(Judg. 8:32)

Thus the children of Israel did not remember God...
(Judg. 8:34)

God Gets Angry

Abimelech arose to defeat Israel.
He judged twenty-three years and died.
After him Jair ruled twenty years.
He was called a Gileadite.

And the children of Israel did evil again
in the sight of the Lord.
The anger of the Lord was hot against them.
God showed them He could be hard.

He delivered them into the hands of the Philistines.
And they were vexed and so oppressed,
they cried again unto the Lord,
saying "Save us—we are so distressed."

The Lord answered, "You have forsaken Me,
and I will deliver you no more.
Go to the gods you have chosen."
My God was really sore.

So they put away the strange gods;
they put them away from them.
Back they came unto the Lord.
His soul grieved, and they came back to Him.

(Judg. 10)

Samson

And the children of Israel did evil again in sight
of the Lord; and the Lord delivered them into
the hand of the Philistines forty years
(Judg. 13:1)

An angel appeared to the woman.
This is what he spoke—
"You, who is barren now, shall bear a son.
Listen now, for this is no joke.

"Stay away from wine and similar drinks,
and your food must be clean.
You will have a special son,
so you can't eat just anything.

"This child cannot have a razor
come upon his little head.
He shall be blessed in your womb.
He must not be near things dead.

"He shall be a deliverer of Israel
from the hands of the Philistines.
He is to be consecrated to the Lord—
that's what this new life means."

So the woman bore a son.
He was called Samson—his given name.
He was blessed by the Lord from birth
in wondrous and amazing fame.

With the jawbone of an ass,
this mighty man slew a thousand men.
He was so powerful, that is,
when he stayed away from sin.

Samson's Wife

One of Samson's vows was not
to go near anything dead.
Samson disobeyed this vow,
and he went right ahead.

He killed a lion, and to this dead
carcass there came bees.
The honey that they left inside,
Samson ate it as he pleased.

When it came to women,
Well, he just never learned.
A little weeping from his wife,
and he would fall for her charm.

To her father he posed this riddle—
Out of the eater, came something to eat;
Out of the strong, came something sweet.

He told the answer to his wife,
which was the lion he slay.
She told the answer to her father,
so Samson lost that way.

Samson betrayed by his wife,
well, he then went back home.
You'll find as you read on that
he just couldn't leave women alone.

(Judg. 14)

Samson and Delilah

Samson came to Gaza and met a harlot there.
When the men were told this, they lay in wait real near.
Then Philistines got tired of Samson; they had to think of a way
to find out where his strength lies, so they could make him pay.

When Samson met Delilah, he fell head over heels in love.
She had the means within her to make him gentle as a dove.
The Philistines paid her money to find
out where his strength lies.
Then they could overcome him, and really tan his hide.

Delilah thought it over and decided she'd get rich.
She worked on Samson and scratched his every itch.
She asked, and he told her one lie after another.
But she kept on trying, until Samson cried "Oh brother."

Well, my friends, to make a long story short,
Delilah found out his secret, because she had his heart.
She told the Philistines after she had cut his hair,
"Now you can overcome him," and she was out of there.

The Lord departed from Samson; the Philistines took his sight.
They made him push a grinder; well, they didn't treat him right.
Soon Samson's hair grew back, and he was strong again.
He, at one of their parties, along with himself killed lots of men.

Samson, in his own death, killed more
Philistines then he had in life.
Although blind, Samson learned to keep the Lord in his "sight."

Then Samson said, "Let me die with the Philistines...
(Judg.16:30)

RUTH

Naomi and Ruth

And it came to pass, there was a famine in the land.
In Bethlehem-Judah there was a certain man.

He went to live temporary in Moab
along with his wife and two sons.
Unfortunately the men all died
and left her with no one.

Naomi had two daughters-in-law;
they were her sons' wives.
They had to do something,
since they were yet alive.

So Naomi called them to her,
and this is what she said—
"You must go home to your people.
Tell them your husbands are dead."

Orpah went back to her people,
but Ruth told her "No,
wherever you live, I will live,
and I'll go wherever you go."

And Ruth said, intreat me not to leave thee,
or return from following after thee, for whither thou
goest I will go, and where thou lodge I will lodge;
thy people shall be my people, and thy God my God.
(Ruth 1:16)

Ruth and Boaz

Now Naomi had a kinsman—
a mighty, wealthy man.
Ruth then asked Naomi,
"Is it all right to work his land?'

While Ruth was gleaming in the fields,
her beauty sure stood out.
She caught the eye of Boaz, her kinsman,
who wanted to know what she was about.

Behold, he came to the field, and said,
"Whose damsel is this?"
She came from the Moab country
with Naomi, to gather what we miss.

And Boaz said unto her,
"You are more than welcome to stay.
I have heard how you treat Naomi,
so I will not send you away."

Ruth, the Moabitess woman,
found favor in her kinsman's eye.
He did what he had to do
to claim her as his beautiful wife.

(Ruth 4:17)

1 SAMUEL

Hannah

Hannah asked the Lord
if He would give her a son.
She would dedicate his life to God
if God would give her one.

Hannah prayed in silence.
Her lips never moved.
Eli saw her praying and may
have thought her full of booze.

God heard her cries, and He
granted her her wish.
She had a healthy son,
and it went without a hitch.

She knew as she nursed him,
soon he'd have to go.
"After I have weaned him,
I will make it so."

She brought the child to Eli.
Lending him to the Lord was her choice.
She prayed, sang, and praised God,
and let her heart rejoice.

(1 Sam.)

Samuel Grew

Samuel was the name of Hannah's child.
She only saw him once a year.
She brought him a little robe when they sacrificed.
The Lord had Hannah's ear.

He blessed her and her husband
for the sacrifice that they had done.
He gave her two daughters.
She was blessed with three more sons.

Samuel lived with Eli in the tabernacle,
where Eli's sons did so much evil;
they listened not to their father's warnings,
because they were full of the devil.

God called Samuel as a boy,
and he answered "Here am I."
He listened to what God had to say.
Then God called him to prophesy.

The child, Samuel, grew in stature,
and in favor with God and men.
An angel appeared before old Eli and told
Him that his sons grew fat with sin.

God told Eli that his sons shall die.
Yes, He said both of them.
This shall be punishment from God
for them not serving Him.

Eli was ninety-eight years old...
(1 Sam. 4:15)

... and he had judged Israel forty years
(1 Sam. 4:18)

The Ark of God

The Philistines captured the Ark of God;
they carried it away from its place;
took it to the house of Dagon.
It made Dagon fall on its face.

Wherever they would take it,
it caused pain and deadly destruction.
Every city that took it,
that city could no longer function.

So they decided after seven months
to return it back to the Israelites.
They asked them to take it back
so it would relieve their plight.

The Lord struck down many men;
there was a great slaughter,
because they looked into the Ark.
Now they know they should not have.

... the Ark of the God of Israel shall not abide with us,
for His hand is sore upon us, and upon Dagon our god.
(1 Sam. 5:7)

Samuel Judged

Now Samuel judged Israel;
he told them to put away false gods.
Teaching them to follow our Lord,
it was proving to be a hard job.

The hands of the Lord were with Samuel
against the Philistines all the days of his life.
He built an altar to our God.
You see, Samuel did things right.

Now when Samuel got old,
he made judges of his sons.
They did not walk as Samuel did,
or serve God as Samuel had done.

The people cried, "Give us a king,
for your sons walk not as you do.
Give us a king. We need a king
to rule us. Please, we're asking you."

Nevertheless the people refused to obey the voice of Samuel,
and they said, "no" but we will have a King over us
(1 Sam. 8:19)

King Saul

There was a young man named Saul,
who was handsome, and he was tall.

His father sent him to find some lost donkeys.
He sought a seer to find what he seeks.

The Lord already had spoken to Samuel saying,
"Tomorrow I'll send you a man
who will rule over my people."
So Samuel anointed Saul to command.

After Saul prophesied, he was proclaimed king.
And all the people shouted, "Long live the king."

The people were satisfied indeed.
"The new king is all that we need."

(1 Sam. 10:1-24)

Saul Messed Up

The Philistines gathered—thousands
and thousands of them to fight.
That gave the Israelite people
such an awesome fright.

The people were distressed.
They hid in caves and behind rocks.
Saul made some offerings to God;.
he did something that he should not.

Samuel asked King Saul,
"What have you done?
Offerings offered to God
can't be done by just anyone."

Then he said to Saul,
"You have done a foolish thing.
You have not kept God's commandment,
even though you are the king.

"You were to be God's chosen.
Your kingdom was to last forever.
But now you've blown it.
What you did was not too clever.

"Now God shall seek a man—
one after His own heart—
a true man of God,
not only handsome, but smart."

But now thy kingdom shall not continue.
The Lord hath sought Him a man after His own heart...
(1 Sam. 13:14)

And there was sore war against the
Philistines all the days of Saul...
(1 Sam. 14:52)

David is Chosen

The Lord rejected King Saul, because
Saul did evil in God's sight.
He did not keep in mind that
to obey is better than sacrifice.

The Lord then sent Samuel to
tell King Saul, that he had to go.
"Why, didn't you obey the Lord?
Only you must know.

"Because you have rejected the work,
God has rejected you as king."
Samuel turned his back on Saul,
but Samuel grieved over this thing.

The Lord called Samuel to fill his horn
with oil, and go to see a man.
"Among his fine sons, you'll find
the next king of my command.

"Do not look at the outward appearances,
for God looks at the heart."
Samuel looked at the firstborn son,
but that was just the start.

Since the Lord has not chose these seven,
there has to be another one.
Jesse then sent for David, the sheep-keeper;
it was his youngest son.

David was a bright-eyed,
good-looking, ruddy lad.
Samuel poured his oil on David's head.
God had chosen, oh yes, He had.

David and Goliath

David was a shepherd boy, who
also took his brothers food.
His father asked him if he
would also bring back the news.

On the side of the Philistines,
there was a mighty, big man.
His name was Goliath, and
he stood six cubits and a span.

He would stand outside the Israeli
camp and bellow out each day.
This scared the Israeli's army;
they were plain dismayed.

Then one day David, the shepherd boy,
came into the Israeli camp.
He heard what King Saul offered him
if he could kill that scamp.

David, with his faith in God,
took his sling and a few rocks.
All it took was one of them
to make the big man drop.

And David behaved himself wisely in all his
ways; and the Lord was with him
(1 Sam. 18:14)

Run David Run

"Run, David, run; Saul is after you.
Hide, David, hide; if he finds you, you're through.

"I know in your heart, he'll always be your king.
He has an evil spirit in him, that's why he treats you so mean."

"Tell me, King Saul, for I don't understand—
you showed me such love, when I slay the giant man.

"And as a boy, it seems, I could do no wrong.
Now, you want to kill me, now that I am grown.

"The Lord has delivered you into my hands twice.
If I wanted to, I could have taken your life.

"But you are my king, and you will always be so.
Why you want me dead is for only you to know.

"So I run and I hide, for I am in God's hand.
I know I am His chosen one—why can't you understand?"

Run, David, run.

And Samuel died...
(1 Sam. 25:1)

David and Abigail

Now, there was a very rich man in Carmel;
his name was Nabal, and his wife was Abigail.

She was a good woman, who was beautiful too.
But he was evil and harsh in what he would do.

David sent ten men to Nabal in his name
to ask him for a favor.
But Nabal sent them back without,
because his salt had lost it's savor.

When Abigail heard this, she made haste
to send them plenty of food.
David just couldn't believe that Nabal
would be so very cruel.

"He has repaid me evil for good,
so I will spare him not."
But Abigail begged, and David heard her;
then he spared the whole lot.

Ten days later, God struck Nabal,
and the evil man died.
David proposed to Abigail,
and she became his wife.

The Death of Saul

Now the Philistines fought Israel,
and the army of the Israeli's fled.
The Philistines followed after them
until all of Saul's sons were dead.

The battle became fierce against Saul.
Soon he was wounded severely.
Saul asked his armor-bearer, "Please
draw a sword through me."

The armor-bearer could not do it,
so Saul fell on his sword himself.
They were all dead now;
none of his sons were left.

When his armor-bearer saw Saul,
he did likewise on his sword.
The Philistines took the cities,
for they were left without a guard.

(1 Sam. 31:1-13)

2 SAMUEL

King of Judah

Seven years and six months, David
was king of Judah alone,
for the house of Judah was the
tribe where David called his home.

There was a long war between the house
of David and the house of Saul.
David grew stronger, while Saul's house
grew weaker, for David was God's call.

David was thirty years old, when
he became Israel's king.
God, as He promised, delivered into
his hands all of the Philistines.

Now, while these things were happening,
David was fathering kids.
He was a righteous man that God rewarded,
and his rewards were something big.

*And David went on and grew great, and
the Lord of Host was with him*
(2 Sam. 5:10)

Michal

Although King David was a mighty warrior,
he loved dancing to the Lord.
His music was by tambourine,
cymbals, psalteries, and harp.

When they brought the Ark up,
there was shouting, and the trumpets blew.
Saul's daughter watched David dance,
and thought, "David, I hate you."

After the offerings to God, David
blessed the people then.
A cake of bread, a piece of meat,
a flagon of wine, to each he did send.

Michal told David he was shameful
dancing before the servants that way.
And she bore no children at all
unto her dying day.

David told Michal, "It's before
the Lord that I play.
He chose me to be ruler,
and this I cannot repay."

(2 Sam. 6:21-23)

David's House

David wanted to build God a house,
but God would build David one.
David had no choice but to
let God's will be done.

And it came to pass, as David sat in
his grand house, the Lord gave him rest.
He thought it's time to build a place
for God's Ark, for it deserves the best.

But the Lord spoke through Nathan;
He said "This is not the time.
I will appoint a place for my house,
but the builder is not thine.

"I shall sat up your seed
after you are gone.
He shall build a house in My name,
for My Ark to call home."

David spoke to the Lord and said,
"You have made me great
according to thine own heart,
and for Thy Word's sake."

So David's house was blessed,
and his love for God was true.
Put your trust in this same God,
and see what he'll do for you.

(2 Sam. 7:1-29)

David and Bathsheba

Then it came to pass one day,
as King David walked around,
he saw from his rooftop,
the prettiest woman in town.

He watched her as she bathed;
she was beautiful to look upon.
He sent for her; they made love; then David sent her home.

Bathsheba conceived and told
King David, "I am with child."
David sent for her husband to come home
to be with her for a while.

But Uriah, her husband,
well, he did not go home.
David thought this won't do,
for our secret will be known.

So King David had another plan—
he sent Uriah to the front line,
which displeased our Lord God, and
David was punished in due time.

(2 Sam.11)

Nathan's Parable

David's sin with Bathsheba displeased
the Lord greatly. So He sent Nathan to him.
Nathan told David of a parable that
told of things outside God's realm.

He spoke of a rich man who had
many flocks and many herds,
and of a poor man with one ewe lamb
that he brought up and nursed.

This poor man loved his ewe.
She ate and drank from his own cup.
Just like it was his very own child,
was the way he raised her up.

Now, a traveler came to the rich man's
House, but he spared his own flock,
and took the poor man's precious little lamb,
and served her in his stock.

David was outraged that he would do such
a bad thing, for he didn't understand.
"You have done this thing, David.
Thou art the man.

"You have many wives, but you took
Bathsheba unto you as wife.
Not only did you take her, but
you also took her husband's life."

(2 Sam. 12)

Absalom's Conspiracy

After the king forgave Absalom and
let him come back home, it came to pass,
Absalom prepared chariots, horses, and men—
an army of followers he did mast.

He stood beside the way of the gate
and charmed the hearts of men.
He judged those that sought the king,
and they quite frankly were taken in.

After forty years, he asked the king to
let him return to Hebron. There he did reign;
the people increased continually with Absalom;
and his conspiracy grew in fame.

Behold, it came to David that Absalom
had Israel's men's hearts.
So his servants with him in Jerusalem
made arrangements for them to depart.

King David left with all his household,
except ten concubines to keep the house.
He left spies behind to keep him informed,
while he remained in exile.

(2 Sam. 15)

Absalom

Run, David, run; your son
Absalom is after you.
And if he catches you, King David,
kill you is what he'll do.

He has many people on his side
who want to make him king.
But you know for a fact
that God is not in that thing.

There will be a battle, and
thousands must die.
You will conquer Absalom.
We know where his fate lies.

He rode under a tree;
he was hanging, yet alive,
until Joab struck him with his sword,
and there Absalom died.

Two men came running
to tell King David the news.
David mourned for his son, Absalom,
for death he did not choose.

(2 Sam. 18)

1 KINGS

Solomon Made King

Now King David was very old
and on his dying bed.
His son Adonijah took in upon himsel
to be king in his brother's stead.

He gathered up some people
who thought they would make it so;
left out Nathan, Zadok, and Solomon,
for he didn't want them to know.

Now, when Nathan heard this, he
went to Bathsheba with a plan.
"Go before King David now.
You must make him understand.

"Although he promised Solomon,
Adonijah has exalted himself as king.
Make him understand i
he does not want this thing."

Although weak, King David called
his son Solomon to his side.
"Put him on my mule at once.
It's time he took a ride."

King Solomon was blessed
and established on the throne.
He loved the Lord as did David.
He was put where he belonged.

So King Solomon sent and they brought him down...
and Solomon said unto him, "Go to thine house."
(1 Kings 1:53)

Solomon's Wisdom

Solomon loved the Lord, walked in the
statues of David, and burnt incenses in high places.
Solomon went to Gibeon—the great high place,
and burnt thousands of offerings that were sacred.

In Gibeon, the Lord appeared unto Solomon in
a dream and asked, "What shall I give thee?"
He answered, "You have given so much to my
father, David—what can I ask for me?

"You have given me, his son, to sit
on this throne as it is this day.
What more can I ask for the people,
except to lead them in your way.

"So give thy servant an understanding heart,
that I may discern between good and bad.
Help me judge them fairly, Lord,
every man, woman, every lass and lad."

This pleased the Lord that Solomon has
asked for this, and not riches and long life.
He made him wise and understanding;
gave him the ability to judge things right.

He also gave him riches and honor
like no other king has had before.
For the rest of his days this is what
King Solomon had in store.

(1 Kings 3:3-12)

God's House

So Solomon was king over Israel,
and God's wisdom was in him.
The babies' mothers—well, he made the
right choice between the two of them.

King Solomon reigned over all
the kingdoms, and was served all his days.
People came from far and near to
see him reign in his God's ways.

His wisdom was so well-known;
even kings admired his work.
He spoke of trees, beast, fowl, and fish.
He was the wisest man on earth.

Then King Solomon saw there
was peace all around;
said, "In the name of God, and unto
David, I must build my father's house now."

It took Solomon seven years,
but Solomon finished it.
What a grand and wondrous place,
for our Lord God's Ark to fit.

... for the glory of the Lord had filled the house of the Lord
(1 Kings 8:10)

Queen of Sheba

When the Queen of Sheba heard
of King Solomon's fame,
she decided she would go see if he
could live up to his name.

She came to Jerusalem, her
camels loaded down with stuff—
gold, spices, and precious stones—
you will never see so much.

She came with questions she
thought that he wouldn't know.
He, of course, answered them all.
He put on a real good show.

She had to see with her own eyes
in order for her to believe it.
All the wonder that he showed to her,
she believed him every bit.

So she went back home with gifts.
She was happy with what she saw.
All her desires were fulfilled.
She was indeed in awe.

(1 Kings 10)

King Solomon's Death

King Solomon was a mighty man
who had seven hundred wives.
He loved many strange women;
he had three hundred concubines.

Then it came to pass,
as King Solomon grew old,
his wives turned to other gods;
Solomon's love for God grew cold.

And King Solomon did evil
in the sight of the Lord.
God grew angry at the king, and
God's punishment was hard.

He said he would afflict the
seed of David, but not for always.
Solomon was king of Israel
until his dying day.

And Solomon slept with his fathers and was buried...
(1 Kings 11:43)

Jeroboam

Jeroboam, Solomon's servant, lifted
his hands up against the king.
He was a mighty man of valor and
industriousness, and Solomon saw these things.

Solomon made him ruler over all
the charge of Joseph's house.
Although clad in new garment, when
the prophet Ahijah found him in a field, they had it out.

Ahijah caught the new garment he wore, and
rent it into twelve pieces, but kept two.
Thus said the Lord, "I will give you ten tribes
out of the land of Solomon,—this I give to you.

But he shall have one tribe for his
father, David's sake, and also Jerusalem's sake,
for he has served false gods instead of Me,
and this has changed his fate."

And the time Solomon ruled over Israel
was forty years, until he died.
His son, Rehoboam, ruled in his stead,
but he only had one tribe.

(1 Kings 12)

Kings

When King Solomon died, his son,
Rehoboam, reigned in his place.
At forty-one, he ruled seventeen years,
in sin and in disgrace.

In the fifth year of King Rehoboam, Egypt took
away treasure, including Solomon's gold shields.
There was war between the kings,
who walked not in God's will.

Abyam, the next king, only reigned
three years in his father's sins.
Then came Asa, who loved God,
and God's heart he did win.

Jehoshaphat, Asa's good son—
he did good in the sight of God.
He also won God's blessings,
for he did a real good job.

In the thirty-eighth year of Asa,
Ahab reigned king of Israel twenty-two years.
With his wife, Jezebel, at his side,
their evil brought the people many tears.

... Ahab did more to provoke God to
anger, than all those before him.
(1 Kings 16:33)

Run, Elijah, Run

Run, Elijah, run; Jezebel is after you.
She is slaughtering the
prophets of God, and she
wants to kill you too.

God said, "Go and hide near the brook.
I'll send the ravens to bring you food.
Drink the water in the brook.
Stay there until I say move.

"The water in the brook dried up,
and now it's time to go.
Find the widow in the town—
she will feed you, because I said so.

"I'll stretch the flour and the oil,
so you can eat for a long time.
Just do as I say, do because
I always take care of mine."

(1 Kings 17:1-10)

The Widow

"I'm gathering these few little sticks
to cook all that I have left,
to feed my child so we can die,
and also to feed myself.

"Yes, I will share with you our water—
sure, you can have a drink.
But the morsel that you asked to share
is much harder than you may think."

The widow said, "I have a child. Why
should I feed this strange man?
My son and I have so little left,
but I must obey his command.

"Something inside me way down deep—
down deep within my heart
tells me to do as he asks,
for to obey would be real smart."

(1 Kings 17:10-24)

Angry Jezebel

When King Ahab told Jezebel all that
Elijah had done, she was some kind of hot;
she had slaughtered all the prophets,
whether they be Elijah or not.

When Elijah heard the message
that Jezebel and Ahab sent to him,
he ran for his life, because
he was afraid of them.

He fell asleep under a broom tree,
and unto him an angel appeared;
said "Eat and drink—I have brought you food
for your journey out of here."

The angel came a second time;
told him to eat some more.
"You must be strong to stand before God—
that's what he wants you for."

Elijah went to the mountains,
and there was a mighty wind;
then an earthquake, and fire,
but God was not in them then.

After the fire, Elijah heard
a small, still voice—
a voice that when you hear it,
you just have to rejoice.

God was speaking to him,
and He sent him on his way.
He had more work ahead of him;
He had a lot to say.

(1 Kings 19)

Naboth's Vineyard

And it came to pass that Naboth had
a vineyard close to Ahab's palace.
He asked Naboth to sell it to him.
"No," he answered, and not out of malice.

Jezebel stepped in, and she
did another thing or two;
called Naboth a blasphemer;
said, "I'll do what I have to do."

They stoned poor Naboth.
Then Ahab took his land.
The word came to Elijah that
they had killed this good man.

Thus said the Lord, "Where dogs licked
Naboth's blood, in that place
dogs shall lick Ahab's blood."
Remember, God's enemies are not safe.

"And Jezebel," said the Lord,
"dogs shall eat her by the wall.
You see, her sins are many,
but I won't list them all."

Ahab, when he heard this, began
to rend his clothes and fast.
He humbled himself before God.
Then God gave him a brief pass.

King Ahab was shot by an arrow
through his heart, and he was dead.
Where they washed his chariot, dogs
licked his blood, as the Lord had said.

(1 Kings 21)

2 KINGS

Elijah and the Fifty

Then Moab rebelled against Israel after the death of Ahab
(2 Kings 1:1)

The king fell down in his chamber
and was sick. "Required if he should die?"—
he asked this of false gods. So God said
he would and that was the reason why.

The angel of the Lord sent Elijah
to meet the messengers of the king.
"Because you inquire of false gods,
sure death shall be your thing."

They returned to the king, and he
asked them why they had come back.
"We met a man of the true God,
who says you will die, and that is that."

The king then sent fifty men to Elijah,
who said, "Thy man of God, come down."
Elijah called fire down from heaven,
and they were no longer around.

Again came another fifty, then fifty
more to die this same way.
The third captain prayed, and lived
to see yet another day.

(2 Kings 1)

So he died according to the word of the
Lord which Elijah had spoken...
(2 Kings 1:17)

Elijah's Whirlwind

And it came to pass that the Lord would
take Elijah into heaven by a whirlwind.
He prepared Elisha to take his place
and to lead the others then.

Fifty men—sons of the prophets—stood
afar off by the Jordan that day.
Elijah took off his mantle, wrapped it,
and smote the water, and divided it that way.

They then passed over on dry land,
and it came to pass,
"What is it I can do for you?"
is what Elijah asked.

Elisha answered, "Give me a double
portion of thy spirit—let it be on me."
"Thou has asked a hard thing, nevertheless
if you see me taken away, so shall it be."

Soon it came to pass, there appeared
horses and a chariot of fire.
Elijah went up by a whirlwind,
and he ascended higher and higher.

(2 Kings 2)

He took up also the mantle of Elijah that fell from him,
and went back, and stood by the banks of Jordan.
(2 Kings 2:13)

Naaman

Naaman was a great captain—a
warrior of the king of host—
an honorable man, a mighty man,
whose leprosy left him as white as a ghost.

There was a little maid, captured out
of Israel and given to Naaman's wife;
said to her mistress, "One day my lord
can heal him—he can make it right."

So the king of Syria sent Naaman
with a letter to Israel's king,
saying "I will pay you lots of stuff

if you can cure this thing."

The king was in a tizzy—"How can I do this?
I am certainly not the Lord."
Elisha came forward and told the king,
for God this is not too hard.

He told Naaman to go to Jordan river,
wash seven times, and be clean.
But Naaman went away angry, saying
"This can't be what he means.

"The rivers where I came from are
much better than this one."
His servants talked to him, and then
he went ahead and got it done.

He went in as a leper; came out
clean with a baby's skin.
Learn how to trust the Word of

God, and be healed, my friend.

One of Elisha's servants got greedy and
tried to get the reward that was turned down,
but ended up with something worst—
Naaman's leprosy all around.

The leprosy therefore of Naaman shall cleave unto thee...
... and he went out from his presence
a leper as white as snow.
(2 Kings 5:27)

Good News

Four lepers sat outside the gate.
They were hungry and prepared to die,
when one said, "Let us go to the enemy;
surrender ourselves. Can't hurt to try."

So that morning they entered the Syrian's camp.
"Either they will kill us, maybe not."
But when they entered their tents,
my! what a surprise they got.

No one was there at all.
No, the enemy had fled.
They heard the sounds of the Lord God;
they ran leaving what they had.

The lepers ate to full;
then they went from tent to tent,
carrying away gold, silver, and food,
until they realized what this meant.

They went back to the gate, to tell the
king the good news, for it was time to share.
"Come on and get the goods,
for the enemy is no longer there."

(2 Kings 7)

Death of the Witch

When Jehu, the son of Jehoshaphat, became
king, he slayed Ahab's family left around.
No one would be left to bury Jezebel—
what was left of her after the hounds.

Jezebel painted her face and
tied her hair back on her head.
She got ready to die when
she heard all her family was dead.

She stood at the window of Naboth's
land—yes, the very same wall.
They threw her out the window;
the witch had a very bad fall.

When they went to bury this cursed woman,
only her feet, hands, and skull were left.
Dogs had eaten her flesh and drank her blood.
She now felt God's holy wrath.

Mourn not for Jezebel, though,
for she was a total witch.
She did evil in the sight of God,
and she could only end like this.

(2 Kings 9:33)

Elisha's Death

Elisha fell sick with the illness
of which he would die.
King Joash came and wept
where Elisha did lie.

Elisha told him, "Take the arrow,
and we must hold the bow."
They shot it out the window; then
Elisha told him what he must know.

He said to the king, "Take the arrow,
then to strike the ground."
He struck it only three times,
then Elisha said with a frown,

"You have smote the ground only three times,
when it should have been five or six.
Now you have really done it—
put yourself in quite a fix."

So Elisha died, and he was buried
in his grave; he turned to bones.
A dead man put into his grave, revived,
stood up, and was gone.

(2 Kings 13)

1 CHRONICLES

The Record

From Adam to David, from Jesse to Jesus,
there were a lot of begotten.
1 Chronicles's first chapter lists all the sons;
most of the girls are forgotten.

From the family of Judah came Jabaz—
an honorable man who loved God.
His mother called him Jabaz, because
giving birth to him was a hard job.

He requested from God to enlarge his coast,
and that He keep him from evil indeed.
God granted him his request and
supplied him all his needs.

God got angry when Uzza tried
to hold up the Ark as it fell.
He smote him, putting fear into David—
he was left to tell the tale.

So he left the Ark with Obededon,
and how his family was blessed—
three months he had it in his place,
and all he had blossomed at best.

So all of Israel was recorded by genealogies,
And behold, it is written in the book.
To learn of each tribe in our Bible,
well, take the time and have a look.

(1 Chron. 1-9)

David's Army

David was in a cave, with the Philistines
encamped in the valley below.
Three of the captains were with him,
ready to go where he said to go.

Now, King David longed for and said,
"O that one would give me a drink."
The three captains broke through the lines;
got him water as quick as a wink.

But, David, he would not drink it.
He poured it out to the Lord.
Said he, "My God forbid me to drink
the blood of those who has worked so hard."

Some of the sons of Benjamin and Judah
came to David in his stronghold.
When the Spirit came upon the chie
of captains, serving David was now his goal.

"We are on your side, son of Jesse.
Peace be unto thee.
We know God helps you.
You are blessed, and we also can be."

There came to David many men
of valour, until there was a great host.
They gave David their allegiance,
because they loved him the most.

(1 Chron. :11-12)

A Warrior Messed Up

King David was a mighty warrior who
killed the Syrians—forty-seven thousand men—
seven thousand who fought in chariots,
and forty thousand who were footmen.

And there came a time that David stayed at
Jerusalem, while Joab went out to fight.
David took their king's crown off his head—
this gold with precious stones crown, a beautiful sight.

He fought a war at Gath, where there was
a man of great stature with many fingers and toes—
six on each hand and six on each foot—
a son of a giant, so this story goes.

Those born unto the giants fell by the hands
of David and by David's servants.
Satan stood up against Israel and provoked
David to number Israel—this was not godsend.

Then the Lord sent pestilence upon Israel
and hundreds of thousands of men.
David prayed unto the Lord for forgiveness
for being foolish and committing this sin.

(1 Chron. :20-21)

So the Lord sent pestilence upon Israel:
and there fell of Israel seventy thousand men...
(1 Chron. 21:14)

2 CHRONICLES

Solomon—Son of David

Solomon, son of David, became king, and
God magnified him and strengthened his kingdom.
King Solomon and all the congregation praised
God, but His Ark remained in a tent in Jerusalem.

Solomon went to the brazen altar before the Lord
and offered a thousand burnt offerings upon it.
In the night God appeared to him; said,
"Whatever you want, you shall get."

Solomon said, "You have given me much
already, mercy, and made me a great king.
Give me wisdom and knowledge so that
I may rule—please grant me this thing."

God said, "Because this is in your heart,
not greed, nor the lives of your enemies,
I shall grant you wisdom and knowledge for yourself.
Riches and honor I will give thee.

"You shall have honors such as no king has
ever known before you, or after you as well."
Solomon came back from his journey to rule
the people, with a great word to tell.

(2 Chron. 1)

A Magnificent House

King Solomon built God's temple—
it was a magnificent house to see.
They brought up the Ark and holy furnishing,
where only priest were allowed to be.

Then the Levite singers
began to sing as one.
The voices, trumpets, cymbals, and harps
blended into a perfectly beautiful song.

"For He is good, for His mercy endures
forever"—they sang this very loud.
As they sang, the house of the Lord
was filled with a holy cloud.

The priest could not continue
because of the holy cloud.
The glory of the Lord
filled up God's holy house.

(2 Chron. 5:13-14)

Then said Solomon, "The Lord hath said that
He would dwell in the thick darkness, but I have
built a house of habitation for thee… forever
(2 Chron. 6:1-2)

When the Queen Came

When the queen of Sheba heard of King Solomon's
Fame, she came to make him prove it.
She brought spices, gold, precious stones,
and questions. Solomon's answers were a hit.

He answered all her questions—
there was nothing he held back that day.
When the queen saw the wisdom of Solomon
and his house, she marveled at what he did say.

She blessed him by his God, that He gave him
wisdom that exceeded the fame she'd heard.
"God has made you king over His people,
and in you established His Word."

She showered him with gifts of gold talents
and great spices, like none ever seen.
King Solomon gave to the queen of Sheba
great wisdom and all the desires of the queen.

So she departed with all her servants;
went back to where she belonged.
A queen quite satisfied with King Solomon,
very happily she went home.

(2 Chron. 9)

*And King Solomon gave to the queen of Sheba
all her desires, whatsoever she asked...*
(2 Chron. 9:12)

EZRA

Building the Temple

... the Lord stirred up the spirit of Cyrus,
King of Persia that he made a proclamation...
... He has charged me to build Him a house at Jerusalem
(Ezra 1:1,3)

Ezra came up from Babylon—a wise man in the laws of Moses.

The people got together round
about the seventh month.
They came together as one, and
there was quite a big bunch.

They offered up to God
offerings both day and night,
even though the people of those
countries gave them quite a fright.

In the second month of the second
year, the work had begun. They laid the foundation
and praised God with song.

Although some of the people cried,
there was also a great shout.
The joy was so great that it
brought the far people out.

(Ezra 3:13)

The Finished Temple

After some ups and downs,
the temple was finally finished.
When the building was complete,
they then had it replenished.

They purified the priest and Levites
together; all of them were pure.
They had a feast for the people of God;
all ate, that's for sure.

They kept the feast of the unleavened bread
seven days with joyful hearts.
Then came Ezra from Babylon;
he came to do his part.

Ezra, who came up from Babylon,
was a wise man in Moses's laws.
He prepared his heart to seek God's laws
and to seek the Lord God's cause.

The king gave Ezra money
to buy whatever he would need
to offer up the offerings of God.
The king made it a decree.

And whatever more shall be needful for the house of
thy God, which thou shall have occasion to bestow,
bestow it out of the king's treasure house.
(Ezra 7:20)

Ezra

When Ezra heard how his people
mingled themselves with people of that land,
he was astonished, so he plucked hair
from his head and beard; he could not understand.

At the evening sacrifice was heaviness
of heart; he fell down on his knees;
called out to God, how ashamed he was.
Believe me, he was not pleased.

"O my God, I am ashamed to
lift up my face to Thee.
Our trespass is grown up, and
we have our iniquities."

When Ezra finished praying, and when
he confessed, he wept.
He called to the mixed people;
told them to separate themselves.

Ezra made Israel swear to do
according to God's law.
He fasted, and he mourned
because of the sin he saw.

And they made an end with all the men, that had
taken strange wives, by the first day of the month.
(Ezra 10:17)

NEHEMIAH

Nehemiah

Nehemiah, a cupbearer to the king,
left that position to serve God instead.
He loved God and his people—
that fact was never hid.

This very important man—
he fasted and he could pray.
Nehemiah confessed his sins before the Lord.
We would call him a prayer warrior today.

He went before the king one day,
and his face was sad.
When the king asked, "What is wrong?
Why are you feeling so bad?"

"Because," said he, "our gates are burned,
and our father's tomb lay in waste,
I would like to return and fix them,
to do whatever it takes."

The King asked him how long it would take
and when shall he return.
It pleased the king to send him
with timber for the gate that burned.

(Neh. 1:1-6)

Nehemiah Teaches the Law

Nehemiah taught the people,
"Do not mourn, nor do weep.
Go your way, eat the fat,
and drink of the sweet.

"Share with those who have not.
Rejoice in great joy, not doubt."
The people went to eat and drink,
and to share with those without.

There was great gladness as the people
made and sat under booths.
Hearing the laws read each day
gave their lives a great boost.

They shouted out and blessed the Lord;
they exalted His name on high—
"You are the Lord who made the heaven
and earth—You are the reason why!"

They told of God's goodness, His blessings,
and the wonderful things He had done.
From Pharaoh to His commandments,
they told of many blessings one by one.

"We write to you today, this sure covenant,
for we are in distress.
Our leaders and priest will seal it.
We will live in it and be blessed.

(Neh. 9 and 10)

ESTHER

Queen Vashti

Queen Vashti—she was so beautiful—
a lady lovely to behold.
When the king sent for her, well,
she refused to do as she was told.

This made the king furious; his
anger burned deep within him.
"What shall I do to Queen Vashti?"
was the question he asked of them.

"This thing Vasthi has done was
not only done just to the king.
She will have all women despising their
husbands and doing all kind of things.

"There must be a royal commandment
written among the laws,
that Vashti no longer can come before you.
This shall go out to all."

Vasthi was dethroned; in other
words, Vashti was gone.
The king sent out for young virgins—
one who could share his throne.

(Esther 1:1-22)

Queen Esther

The king called for beautiful virgins,
so he could find a new queen.
There was a maiden called Esther,
who was chosen for this thing.

She was an orphan who was being
raised by her uncle, Mordecai.
He was the one who took her in
when her mother and father died.

She was among lovely, beautiful women,
but Esther's beauty really stood out.
Hegai, their trainer, gave her special treatment,
which I must say was not his normal route.

He made sure that Esther was in the
best places in the house.
When her turn came to go before the king,
just like that, the king's flame was doused.

The king loved Esther more than
all the other women there.
He took the royal crown,
and he placed it in Esther's hair.

There was a feast given for her.
The king gave her gifts as well as a crown.
This was God's plan for Queen Esther.
God's plans are always sound.

(Esther 2)

Queen Esther's Plight

The king promised Haman he'd
put him in a higher place.
This gave Haman the power
to annihilate the Jewish race.

When Mordecai learned what was to
happen on a certain day—
how his people would be slaughtered
and their possessions taken away,

he tore his garments; put on sackcloth
and ashes; he cried out a bitter cry.
Every province that the king commanded,
Jews prayed, for they didn't want to die.

When Queen Esther heard this,
she was deeply distressed.
Now was the time for her to act—
she was to be put to the test.

She must first fast and pray
for three days and three nights.
The king still didn't know she was Jewish—
now you can imagine Esther's plight.

To go before the king when you have
not been called meant death to those who did.
Esther pleased the king so much, he
offered her the golden scepter instead.

Haman

Haman, with his wife's help, got
what he thought was a good idea—
"We can create a gallows, then
hang Mordecai, the Jew, up there.

"In fact, we can, with the king's
permission, kill all of the Jews."
Haman's hate was so deep for them,
that in his heart hate stewed.

Little did he know that
the king had not forgot.
The king remembered that
Mordecia had foiled an evil plot.

He asked Haman how to reward a man
who deserved special treatment.
Haman, in his heart, decided he was
the man to whom the king meant.

He then suggested that the king give
to him a special robe and horse to ride;
parade him through the city square
for the people to see his pride.

The king said, "Make it so," and
this was done to Mordecai.
Old Haman, well, he just wanted
to go somewhere and hide.

Afterward Mordecia went back
outside to the king's gate,
while Haman hid his face
and brewed in his own hate.

(Esther 6)

The End of Haman

Haman was so happy he was chosen
to go to the king's house to dine.
A feast was prepared for him—
the best food and the best wine.

"Queen Esther," he thought, "has found
favor in me and invited me again.
This time when I get there, I'll
get rid of that awful man."

Now, the king had told Queen Esther
she could have anything she wanted.
"You can have half my kingdom—
you can have it if you want it."

Queen Esther, after fasting and praying,
had something else in mind.
She asked for the lives of her people,
who were to be killed in time.

The king arose in anger; he
got up and left the room.
Haman knew his anger was against him;
now he could only feel doom.

When the king returned, he heard of
Haman's gallows that was fifty cubits high.
"Hang him there, my servants.
Haman must surely die."

Although Haman meant his gallows
for evil, God had another plan.
He will turn evil for good, when
you put things into God's hands.

JOB

Job

Job was a man of God, who was blessed
with cattle and lots of wealth.
He had seven sons and three daughters.
He was blessed also with his health.

Satan saw this man of God, and
thought he could make him sin.
Satan made a deal with God—
one he thought he could win.

God said he could go ahead,
as long as he kept Job alive.
"Go ahead, do your worst.
Job will stay on his God's side."

Job lost his cattle, servants, and kids.
He tore his clothes and shaved his head.
The devil thought he had him,
but he praised God instead.

Then the devil gave him sores and boils
that had pus and lots of pain.
His wife said, "Curse your God, and die.
Can't you see, He's the blame?"

Job stayed strong in God, for
he knew God would not do that.
Because of his strong trust in God,
He gave him his wealth back.

He gave him back his servants;
gave him children too.
Put your trust in God, my friend,
and see what he'll do for you.

(Job 1)

Job—
An Upright Man

Why do we have to suffer, is a
question long been asked.
Job was God's servant, yet he
was put to a terrible test.

Job was a man of wealth, who
trusted God in all things.
He had cattle, donkeys, and children. He
got up early to offer God his burnt offerings.

His seven sons, each on his appointed day,
would host the party at his house.
They would invite their sisters,
and they would all hang out.

One day ole Satan, while going
to and fro through the land,
asked God if he could test Job,
who was a blameless and upright man.

Satan thought if he took
away all that Job had,
he would curse God and sin
if things were going bad.

God said, "Just don't kill him,
but do what you have to do.
Job will still serve Me—
I know his love is true."

(Job 1)

Satan Attacks

Satan attacked Job on every hand.
Job didn't know what hit him.
All his cattle and donkeys were gone;
then his children—he lost all of them.

"Naked I came from the womb,
and naked I shall return.
I bless and I praise you, Lord.
My praises, Lord, You've earned."

Then Satan attacked Job's health—
gave him sores and boils full of pus.
From the soles of his feet to the top
of his head, his body was filled up.

Job was in so much pain,
his wife had had enough.
"Curse your God, and die," she said,
"How can you take so much?"

Job, after so much pain, cursed
the day of his birth—
"If I had only been stillborn, and
had never lived on this earth."

His friends came to see him;
said, "Sin has caused you this pain."
"No," he answered, "I praise my God,
for God wouldn't do these things."

Job's Death

Hearken unto this O Job, stand still and
consider the wondrous works of God.
(Job 37:14)

Touching the Almighty God,
we cannot find Him out.
He is excellent in power and judgment—
of that have no doubt.

Job heard the Lord's voice—
it came to him from a whirlwind.
The Lord answered Job, and
His answer humbled Job again.

God's infinite wisdom and power—
like Him there is no others.
He beholds all high things—His greatness
is so close, they are joined one to another.

Job answered God, then he
repented in ashes and dust.
God was forgiving to Job;
then He returned to him his stuff.

He was blessed with wealth, animals,
three daughters, and seven sons.
Job lived 140 years; he saw
four generations before his life was done.

So Job died being old and full of days
(Job 42:17)

Read all about Job in the book of Job.

PSALMS

Psalms

Help me, oh Lord, in my times of trouble.
Please don't leave me alone.
You are my shield and my glory.
You hear my cries and my every moan.

You were with me when I lay down and slept,
and were with me when I awoke.
I have no fear, for You sustain me,
and all my enemies You have smote.

You have broken the teeth of the ungodly.
Salvation belongs to You.
Your many blessings are upon Your people;
and Your love is ours too.

(Ps. 3)

Confess your sins unto the Lord,
although He already knows.
It's foolish to think you can hide—
He sees you where ever you go.

God forgives our every transgression.
In His Spirit there's no deceit.
Unconfessed sin gives us trouble,
and can only make us weak.

Instruct me in the way I should go,
and always guide me with Thine eyes.
I want to learn the laws of Moses
and to keep them until I die.

(Ps. 32)

I Will Bless the Lord

I will bless the Lord at all times.
In my mouth continually will be praise.
My soul shall brag of the Lord;
the humble shall hear it and be saved.

O, magnify the Lord with me.
Let us exalt His name together.
I sought the Lord, and he heard me;
delivered me from all fears and made me better.

Those who looked to Him were radiant,
And their faces were not ashamed.
The angel of the Lord encamped all
around those who fear Him; deliverance is His aim.

O, taste and see that the Lord is good.
Blessed is the man who trusts in Him.
O, fear the Lord, you, His saints.
Those who fear Him, He will continually bless them.

Come on, you children, I will
teach you the reason why
the eyes of the Lord are on the righteous
and His ears are open to their cry.

(Ps. 34)

Praise the Lord

The idols of the nation are statues
made of silver and gold—
the works of man's hands, but
heathen statues have not a soul.

They have mouths, but speak not;
eyes, but they cannot see;
ears, which can hear nothing;
no breath, so praises they do not need.

Praise the Lord and bless our Savior—
He breathed breath into man.
It is silly to trust a man-made statue.
God's people, make a stand.

Stand up for God and fear Him.
Bless the Lord with every breath.
His mighty name endureth forever.
And in His will you'll find sweet rest.

Praise the Lord.
Praise the Lord.
Praise the Lord.

(Ps. 135:15)

Praise Him Forever

Praise the Lord with the sound of trumpets.
Praise Him with the lute and harp.
Praise Him with the timbre and dance.
Praise God Almighty from your heart.

Praise Him with the loud cymbals;
with the tambourine, piano, and flute.
Praise Him, everybody, from the
oldest to our youth.

Let everyone that has breath praise Him,
for He is worthy to be praised.
His wonders are all around us,
and His love keeps us amazed.

Don't let dry bones praise Jesus for you.
Praise Him for yourself.
He shed His blood and died for us.
He arose and was seen before He left.

Our praise is a sweet aroma
that we know that our God loves.
Praise God now and forever;
He will hear you up above.

Praise Him forever!

(Ps. 150)

PROVERBS

Wisdom and Instruction

To know wisdom and instruction is
to become aware of the teaching.
To receive the instruction of wisdom,
judgment, and equity takes every inkling.

A wise person will hear and increase his
understanding and learn all that he can.
The fear of the Lord is the beginning o
knowledge; so be wise, my fellowman.

For fools despises wisdom and instruction;
don't want to hear what their parents have to say;
willing to listen to sinners that entice them;
letting evil send them to an early grave.

Wisdom cries out for you to hear her;
so don't think you know it all.
Your destruction will come as a whirlwind,
when distress and anguish call.

Hearken to wisdom and live safely.
Be quiet from evil's fear.
Walk in the teachings of reason.
Always keep God's Word in here (heart).

(Prov. 1)

God Hates

God hates a proud look; a lying tongue;
a hand that shed innocent blood of anyone;

a heart that devised wicked thoughts;
fast, mischievous feet that run not where they ought;

a false witness that tells lies;
one who soweth discord by his brother's side.

We must keep His commandments, and
forsake not our mother's law.
Bind them continually in our hearts
with a closed jaw.

Let it keep you wherever you go,
even when you are asleep.
When you are awake, listen
and hear it speak.

For the commandment is a lamp,
and the law is light.
Reproofs of instruction is
the way of life.

(Prov. 5:16-23)

The Harlot's House

My son, keep My words; carry
My commandments inside you.
Keep all My commandments and live.
My laws are important to use.

Call wisdom your sister, and
call understanding your closest kin.
They will keep you from becoming immoral
if they are kept deep within.

Let not the crafty harlot intrigue you
with perfume and scanty dress.
She can bring down the strongest man
and make your life a real mess.

Listen to me, my children;
hear the words of my mouth—
Let not your heart lead you;
stay away from the harlot's house.

Her house is the way to hell.
Did you hear me?—I said hell.
Use your wisdom and understanding;
only you can end this tale.

(Prov. 7)

Receive Wisdom's Instruction

Receive my instruction, and not silver;
knowledge rather than choice gold;
for wisdom is better than rubies—
wisdom leaves them out in the cold.

I, wisdom, live with prudence and witty inventions
that your desires can't be compared with.
The fear of the Lord is to hate evil pride and
Arrogance—these things should make you sick.

Counsel is mine and sound wisdom. I am
Understanding, and I have strength.
By me kings reign and princes decree justice.
Even all the judges, with me, make sense.

I love them that love me, and those that
seek me early shall find me here.
Riches and honor are with me—durable
riches and righteousness without fear.

My fruit is better than gold and my
revenue better than choice silver.
I will cause those that love me to inherit
substance, and fill their treasures—this I will deliver.

(Prov. 7:10-21)

Wisdom

Happy is the man who finds wisdom,
and he that gets understanding.
It is more precious than rubies, gold,
or all those richly things.

She is a tree of life to them
that take hold and retain her worth.
She is happiness, joy, and peace.
The Lord, by wisdom, formed the earth.

By understanding, He has established the heavens.
By His knowledge, depths are broken up
and the clouds drop down the dew.
Wisdom keeps us from being a nut.

If we keep sound wisdom, it will
keep us safe and we will not stumble.
We will not be afraid, because
wisdom helps us to stay humble.

The curse of the Lord is in the house of

the wicked, but He blesses the house of the just.
The wise shall inherit glory.
Wisdom is given to all of us.

(Prov.)

Still More Wisdom

Righteousness is the only way to
deliver us when we are dead.
Treasures of the wicked profit nothing,
is what wise Solomon said.

The memory of the just is blessed,
but the name of the wicked shall rot.
The wise in heart will receive commandments,
but the prating fool shall drop.

He that walks upright walks safely,
but he that winks causes sorrow.
The mouth of the righteous is a well of life
that the wicked can't even borrow.

The tongue of the just is as choice silver,
while the heart of the wicked is little worth.
The lips of the righteous feed many
the Lord's blessing, which cover the earth.

The fear of the Lord prolongs your days,
but the years of the wicked are short.
The hope of the righteous shall be gladness
within our righteous hearts.

(Prov. 10)

Who Can Find a Faithful Man?

Most men will proclaim to us his own
goodness, but who can find a faithful man?
The just man walks in integrity,
as only a faithful man can.

Who can say, "I have made my heart clean.
I am pure from my sin."?
The hearing ear and the seeing eye—
the Lord gave both to men.

Love not sleep, or you'll miss your blessing.
Open your eyes and see.
Open your eyes and get satisfaction.
Be all God wants you to be.

There is gold and a multitude of rubies,
but knowledge is a precious jewel.
Taste not the bread of deceit,
for that will make you seem cruel.

He who goes about revealing secrets,
or he who curse his parents,
your light will be put out in
obscure darkness. Well, you must not dare it.

(Prov. 20)

Merlene Tarver Howard

Who Can Find a Virtuous Wife

Who can find a virtuous wife?
She's worth far more than rubies and such.

She has the heart of her husband,
who has no lack of trust.

She does him good and not evil
all the days of her life,
working willingly with her hands,
trying hard to be a good wife.

She provides food for her household.
She's like the merchant ship,
baking biscuits and frying chicken,
with the baby on her hip.

Her lamp does not go out at night;
she sleeps with an open eye.
If her family is not home yet,
then that's the reason why.

She opens her mouth with wisdom.
On her tongue are words so kind.
She watches over her household.
And you never hear her whine.

Who can find a virtuous woman?
She's worth her weight in gold.
May God bless and keep her.
Dear Lord, bless her soul.

(Prov. 31)

ECCLESIASTES

A Wise King Falls

Even a wise man can sometimes fall—
King Solomon is proof of that.
He no doubt had it all—riches and wisdom—
that is a well-known fact.

He had gold, cattle, and treasures—
whatever his heart desired.
He had sons and daughters from
many wives, that which the king did sire.

He said in his heart, the wise
man's eyes are in his head,
but the fool walks in darkness.
Now dieth the wise man as the fool instead.

For God gives to the man that is good
in sight, wisdom, knowledge, and joy.
But to the sinner what he give,
they can never enjoy.

(Eccles.)

There's a Time

To everything there is a time.
Everything has a season.
A time for every purpose under heaven—
God's time has a reason.

A time to be born, and a time to die;
a time to plant, and a time to sigh;
a time to kill, and a time to heal;
a time to breakdown and a time to build;
a time to weep, and a time to fuss;
a time to mourn when you've had enough;
a time to embrace, and a time to dance;
a time to be loved by our fellow man;
a time to keep, and a time to throw away;
a time for war, then a peaceful day.
God has made everything beautiful in His time,
so man can enjoy. His will be thine.

Whatever God does, it is forever.
Nothing can change that—no, not ever.
God shall judge the righteous as well as the wicked.
There's no time for both, so you must pick it.

(Eccles. 3)

Vanity

Do not let your mouth cause you to sin—
be careful what you vow.
When you make a promise to the Lord,
be ready to keep it somehow.

He that loves money will not be satisfied,
or he that has wealth, and wants more.
Vanity is like a pain in your side,
or like an open sore.

Naked you came into this world,
and naked you shall return.
Take the portion God gave to you—
this is a gift given, not earned.

Vanity is an evil disease—it covers
your life with darkness.
No matter how many years you live,
your life will be one of hardness.

For what has the wise man more than the fool?
Or the poor know how to walk?
Better to wander in God's goodness and glory
than to let vanity talk.

(Eccles. 6:10-20)

Death Comes to Good and Bad

Whatever your hands find to do,
do it with all your might.
There is no work or wisdom in the
grave, nor knowledge, nor device.

For the race is not to the swift,
nor the battle to the strong.
Neither bread to the wise, and
riches, don't just come along.

Man knows not his time—as fish
taken in an evil net;
like birds caught in a snare, man falls
suddenly, and he may not be ready yet.

Wisdom is better than weapons of war.
One sinner destroys much good.
Being wise and understanding will take you
farther then sin ever could.

It is easy for the poor wise man
to not even be remembered.
His quiet wise words are heard,
as the loud fool's words grow dimmer.

(Eccles. 9)

Wisdom is better than weapons of war:
but one sinner destroyed much good.
(Eccles. 9:18)

SONG OF SOLOMON

Black, But Comely

Let him kiss me with the kisses of his
mouth, for your love is better than wine.
The king has brought me into his chambers.
We will be glad, rejoice, and have a good time.

I am black, but comely. Look not upon me,
because the sun has touched me and I am black.
Tell me, O thou, whom my heart loves.
My beloved is into me, and I truly love that.

Behold, thou art fair, my love; behold, thou
art fair. Thou has doves eyes that stare.
Behold, thou art fair, my beloved. Yea,
pleasant beyond compare.

My beloved is like a roe or a young hart.
Behold, he stands behind our wall.
My beloved spake and said unto me,
"Come away, for my heart calls."

(Song of Sol. 1 and 2)

My beloved spake and said unto me, rise up,
my love, my fair one and come away
(Song of Sol. 2:10)

Song of Solomon

To Solomon:

My own vineyard is before me.
You, Solomon, may have a thousand and then.
And to take care of your own fruit,
there may be at least two hundred men.

The Beloved

You live in the garden. The companions
listen to hear you speak.
Let me hear it, for you
you are so unique.

The Shulamite

Make haste, my beloved.
Be a gazelle, or a young stag,
on the mountain of sweet spices,
make haste and be real fast.

(Song of Sol. 8:12-14)

ISAIAH

The Day of the Lord of Host

The day of the Lord of Host shall be
upon every one that is lofty and proud.
Those that be lifted up shall be
brought down to a bow.

The idols God shall utterly abolish.
They shall hide in the rocks and caves,
for fear of the Lord shall cause these
man-made idols to behave in this way.

The day of the Lord will take away finery—
all your gold bracelets and the veils,
the perfume, apparel, and jewelry.
You shall be stinky, rather than a sweet smell.

Woe to him who declare their sin,
and to him that just don't care.
Woe to the ones who reward evil,
and cause God's people to err.

When the Lord washes away the filth
of the daughters and shall purge the blood,
He will deliver the daughters of Zion—
they shall become His well beloved.

(Isa. 3 and 4)

Woe to Strong Drink

Woe to them that rise early in the morning
to have a strong drink,
then continues the rest of the day
not caring what anyone thinks.

They regard not the works of the Lord,
or the operations of His hands.
Hell has enlarged itself to receive
the unclean, brought-down man.

Woe to them that sin
as if it were a big joke.
Woe to him that thinks him wise
in his own eyes—instead he is a dope.

Woe to the mighty men drinking wine
and other strong drinks.
You toss away the work of the Lord
as quick as you can blink.

None shall be weary, nor stumble.
Among them none shall slumber and sleep.
God's hand is stretched out, still His
anger's not turned away from His sheep.

Therefore hell hath enlarged herself,
and opened her mouth without measure:...
(Isa. 5:14)

(Isa. 5)

Look Forward

Look forward to peace, sweet peace
like nothing we have seen,
where the wolf shall lay with the lamb,
as if it were a common thing.

A calf and a bear cub shall frolic,
while the cow and bear share food.
As the lion eat straw like cattle,
led by a child's rules.

They shall not destroy His holy mountain,
but have knowledge as the sea.
In that day of peace and blessings,
Lord, we will please Thee.

Behold, God is my salvation.
Jehovah has my trust.
Call on His great name and praise Him.
His name is exalted on us.

Behold, God is my salvation; I will trust, and not be afraid;
for the Lord Je-Ho'VAH is my strength and my song...
(Isa. 12:2)

(Isa. 11 and 12)

The Fall of Lucifer

How you have fallen, Lucifer,
cut down to the ground,
trying to be more than God.
Now God has sent you down.

The pits of hell have been created
for you, and enlarged for your kind.
It amazes me that so many want to
serve you, and have a carnal mind.

God has stripped you of all you power
and swept you with His broom.
The only powers you possess
are destruction, sin, and doom.

So go back to the pit
that was created for you to reign—
back to the evil that you know,
that will only cause us pain.

*How art thou fallen from heaven, O Lucifer, son
of the morning! How art thou cut down to the
ground, which didst weaken the nation!*
(Isa. 14:12)

(Isa. 14)

Woe to Those Not Trusting Him

"Woe to the rebellious children," said the Lord,
"that do not listen to Me.
They are covered with a covering, not My Spirit.
Their sins are for the world to see.

They've put themselves in the strength
of Pharaoh, and it shall be their shame.
They carry their evil to the wrong people.
They can't help, for their help is in vain.

These rebellious, lying people
will not hear the Lord's law,
nor hear the prophesy of the right things,
nor see what the seers saw.

You shall defile the graven images
of silver and the molten image of gold.
The name of the Lord shall be upon the
mountain—truly a light to behold.

For His name shall burn with
His anger, and with a heavy burden.
His lips and tongue burning as a devouring
fire, of that you can be certain.

Woe to them who do not look to or seek the Lord
but rely on their own works.
God will stretch out His hand, and all
will fall and perish from this earth.

(Isa. 30-31)

Lift Up Your Eyes on High

Lift up your eyes on high.
The Creator faint not, nor is He weary.
Just wait on the Lord, he will renew your strength,
then you will see things more clearly.

Those that wait on the Lord
shall mount up with eagle's wings.
They shall run and not tire—
God gives power to overcome these things.

Fear not for God is with you.
He will hold you with a righteous hand.He will strengthen you
and help you, as only God can.

God will hold up His servants, of whom
He is delighted. He puts His Spirit on them,
for He that created the heaven and earth
and His Holy Spirit walks therein.

He is the Lord, that is His name, and
His glory will not be given to another.
Neither give God's praise to the graven images,
but to Him, and none other.

(Isa. 40-43)

No Other God

Remember not the former things,
neither consider things of old.
I will do a new thing—it shall
spring forth, and you will know.

The beast of the fields shall honor Me.
I will give my water to my chosen.
The people I formed for Myself

shall praise Me—I, the Lord, have spoken.

I am He that will not remember thy sins,
for I have blotted them out.
I Am, the Lord, formed you from the womb,
of that have no doubt.

I am the first; I am the last;
besides Me there is no other.
Fear not, nor be afraid; I am the only God,
and I know no other.

Fear ye not, neither be afraid... is there a God besides Me?
Yea, there is no God; I know not any.
(Isa. 44:8)

The Prophecy of Christ

Isaiah, the Prophet, told of
many things to come.
He told of Christ's coming,
and how He would be God's son.

Isaiah told of how He would
be treated, and it will not be nice;
how He, although innocent,
would be wounded in His sides.

This prophecy tells us how Jesus
would bare the sins of many.
He'll make intercession for our
transgressions, of which there are plenty.

He told of His death, and His burial
in the rich man's tomb;
how He would accept the awful death
so we sinners would not be doomed.

He told of how the Son of God would
be afflicted, and by His stripes we are healed.
All that Christ did for us sinners,
we really got quite a deal.

We should sing out His praises, and
We should sing them loud and clear.
If not for His sacrifice,
we would not be here.

(Isa. 53)

Daughters of Zion

Women of Zion, go forth as brightness
and salvation; shine as a light;
let everyone see your righteousness;
keep your glory shining bright.

You shall no longer be forsaken, but
shall be a crown of glory.
The Lord rejoices over you,
no matter what your story.

We shall gather and eat of His goodness.
We shall be loud with praise.
We shall drink in the court of His
holiness and be leaders for the unsaved.

Lift up a standard for the people,
daughters of Zion, show them the way.
They shall call us holy people;
our salvation comes with our praise.

They shall call them, the holy people,
the redeemed of the Lord...
(Isa. 62:12)

JEREMIAH

Jeremiah, the Prophet

The Word of God came to Jeremiah, saying
"Before I formed you in the womb, I knew you.
Before you were born, I sanctified you.
I ordained you a prophet; you have My work to do."

I answered Him saying, "Me, Lord?
I can't do it, because I am too young."
God told me I could do it
and it's time to get it done.

"You shall go where I send you;
speak when I say speak.
Be not afraid for I am with you.
I will not leave you weak."

Then the Lord touched my mouth.
This what He said to me—
"I have put words in your mouth;
placed you over nations. Now, what do you see?"

"I see a branch of an almond tree."
"Well done, now what else do you see?"
"I see a boiling pot facing away from the north."
Then God said to me,

"Out of the north, evil shall come
upon all of the land.
I will send judgment against those who
forsake Me and worship gods made with men's hands.

"Go forth in My name. I will strengthen
You, and you will be strong.
Although they shall fight you,
just know that they are wrong.
I will be with you; just go in My name.
Plea with my people; show them that I Am is their aim."

(Jer. 1)

Before I formed thee in the belly I knew thee; and before
thou camest forth out of the womb I sanctified thee,
and I ordained thee a prophet unto the nations.
(Jer. 1:5)

And they shall fight against you; but they
shall not prevail against thee...
(Jer. 1:19)

Hear God's Word

Hear the Word of the Lord; O ye people,
enter into the Lord's house;
amend your ways and your doings;
your sinful ways are not allowed.

Trust not in lying words,
and thoroughly amend your ways.
If you walk in sin, there's no profit;
you will remain, yes, there you will stay.

The Lord has called you—can't you hear Him,
for you answer Him not?
If you provoke Him to anger,
His justice will punish the lot.

He knows you are following idols,
committing adultery with your neighbor's wife.
This is not what God intended, and
God's wrath will take your life.

Hear this now, O foolish people,
who have eyes and do not see,
who have ears and do not listen,
God is asking, "Do you fear Me?"

Neither say they in their hearts,
let us now fear the Lord our God...
(Jer. 5:24)

Hananiah

Hananiah began to prophesy,
and he broke Jeremiah's yoke.
The Word of the Lord spoke to Jeremiah.
These are the word's God spoke—

Jeremiah came to Hananiah and told him,
"Listen to what the Lord has to say.
You have broken the yoke of wood,
but made the yoke of iron instead."

When the prophet prophesied of peace,
and when their words came to pass,
the true prophets will be known,
For God's Word will be cast.

Jeremiah said to Hananiah, "The
Lord has not sent you. You lie;
the people have trusted you.
This year you will surely die."

So Hananiah, the prophet died the same year,
in the seventh month
(Jer. 28:17)

Nothing is too Hard

God's Word came to Jeremiah saying,
"Is there anything too hard for Me?
The Israelite children angered Me, when
they built this city, which caused My fury.

"They just don't listen, and have
turned to Me their backs.
The house they call by my name,
they defiled it just like that.

"They built high places to Baal—
a place I command them not.
Their children shall pass through the fire,
for they have made Me "hot."

"Like I have brought evil upon them,
so will I bring to them the good.
Fields shall be brought in the land
just as I said they would."

These words came to Jeremiah
while still in the prison court,
"Men shall buy fields for money
in the mountains, valleys, and ports."

(Jer. 32)

... and changed his prison garments,
and he did constantly eat bread...
Until the day of his death...
(Jer. 52:33-34)

LAMENTATIONS

God was Angry

God was angry; He was real, real mad.
He cast down from heaven to earth
the beauty of Israel, because
they had behaved so bad.

He cut off every horn.
He has drawn back His right hand.
He swallowed up the strongholds;
no palaces did yet stand.

The law is no more, and
the prophets find no vision.
They have seen false and deceptive vision—
God's anger is the reason.

Cry, cry out loud, and let
you tears run day and night.
Give yourself no relief or rest,
for what you did was not right.

(Lam. 2)

I Called Upon Thy Name

Remembering mine affliction and my misery—
the wormwood and the gall—
my soul still remembers and is humble,
as my hopeful mind recalls.

It is of the Lord's mercies that we are not
consumed, because His compassions fail not—
they are new every morning. He is my portion,
and His faithfulness never stops.

Fear and snare is come upon us; desolation
and destruction cause my eyes to tear.
My eye trickles down without ceasing, until
the Lord from heaven looks down here.

Mine enemies chase after me like a bird,
but they really have no cause.
They cut off my life in the dungeon; they
stoned me, and I am cut off.

I called upon thy name O Lord out of the low dungeon.
(Lam. 3:55)

Restore Us, Lord

Our inheritance has been turned over
to aliens; foreigners live in our houses;
we pay for our water and wood;
we labor from the moment we're aroused.

Our fathers sinned, but are no more,
but we bear their iniquities.
Servants rule us; we risk our lives to
get bread; this has brought us to our knees.

The joy of the heart has ceased; our dance turned
to mourning. Woe to us, we have sinned.
Because of this, our hearts are faint; our eyes
grow dim because of what our fathers did back then.

Turn us back to You, O Lord. Why do
You forsake us for so long a time?
Renew our days of old, unless Your anger
has rejected us until You again call us Thine.

(Lam. 5)

Unless you have utterly rejected us,
and are very angry with us!
(Lam. 5:22)

EZEKIEL

Ezekiel's Vision

The Word of the Lord came to Ezekiel, the
priest; and this is what he saw—
he looked, and behold, a whirlwind
and a brightness that would drop your jaw.

He saw a great cloud and a fire the color
of amber; then out of the fire
came four creatures—the likeness of man—
that would scare us rather than admire.

Everyone of them had four faces, and
everyone of them had four wings.
Their feet had soles of a calf

that sparked, or so it seemed.

They had the hands of a man's on all their wings,
and their wings joined one another.
They also had four faces—
each one different from the other.

One was a man's face,
the second like a lion's face,
the third like a ox, the fourth like an eagle.
Now wouldn't that make your heart race?

Their wings all stretched upward
and covered their bodies.
They all went forward in the spirit,
but they had other qualities.

As for the likeness of the living creatures,
they appeared as burning coals;
the fire was bright; out came lightning;
they appeared like a lightning bolt.

Their work was like it were a wheel—
a wheel in the middle of a wheel.
Where the spirit went they went also;
the spirit in them was real.

There, above them, was the likeness of a
throne, and upon it the appearance of a man.
It appeared as a bright fire around a rainbow.
His words we could understand.

(Ezek. 1)

*... this was the appearance the likeness
of the glory of the Lord...*
(Ezek. 1:28)

Israel's Message

"Son of man," thus said the Lord,
"an end has come to the four corners of the land.
I will send My anger against you;
you tell them, son of man.

"I will judge you according to your ways;
for your abominations you will pay.
My eye will not spare you,
for I have no pity for your way.

"Doom has come to those who live
in the land; none shall remain.
The time has come; the day draws near;
your iniquities are indeed the blame.

"In the day of God's wrath,
they will not satisfy their souls.
With your stumbling blocks of sin,
you can't buy peace with silver or gold.

"I will judge you according to your ways,
and according to what you deserve.
Then you will know that I am God;
you have indeed heard My Word."

(Ezek. 7)

Dry Bones

The Holy Spirit picked up Ezekiel;
carried him into a valley of dry bones.
There were many, and they were very dry,
for all life in them was gone.

God's question to him was, "How
can these dry bones live?"
He answered, "O Lord God, You know
this God who gave life to Adam's rib."

God told Ezekiel to prophesy to the bones—
"Tell them to hear the Word of the Lord.
To these bones I will give breath, so
you shall live and be on guard.

"After breath shall come sinews; then
flesh shall come upon them too.
I shall cover them with skin,
and you shall see what I can do."

Ezekiel prophesied as God told him,
and the bones began to rattle.
The bones came together, bone to bone,
and stood as an army going into battle.

But there was no breath in them—
at least no breath yet.
Ezekiel prophesied as God commanded;
they came alive and drew breath.

(Ezek. 37)

DANIEL

For God is My Judge

Daniel, whose name means "for
God is my judge," and that is how he lived.
Although they changed his name,
they could not change his will.

He served the one and only God,
but he served the king's palace too.
He and his friends—good-looking and smart—
did what they had to do.

They were each given a king's portion
of delicacies and drink,
plus three years of training. With new names,
they tried to change how they did think.

But Daniel purposed in his heart not to
defile himself with the king's portions.
God had brought him into favor,
so he had to proceed with caution.

"I'm sorry, Daniel, but I fear the king,
who has appointed you this food."
"If he sees you guys looking worst than
the others, then he would treat me cruel."

Then said Daniel, "Test us ten days.
Give us vegetables to eat, and let us drink water.
Give to the others their portions,
then see if we look as we oughta."

So he tested them as Daniel asked.
He did a ten-day test.
At the end of the time, he was surprised—
the four of them looked better than the rest.

As for these four children God gave them
knowledge and skills... and Daniel had
understanding in all visions and dreams
(Dan. 1:17)

The King's Golden Image

The king made an image,
and it was made of gold.
When the people heard the music, they
were to bow down as they were told.

Everywhere in the province, all the
most important had to bow.
If they did not do this thing,
the king would know somehow.

Those who did not bow would
be thrown into a fiery furnace.
Shadrach, Meshach, and Abed-Nego could not,
so certain Jews saw that they were punished.

They went to the king and said, "King, they
don't obey you, and we know this is so.
They refuse to bow down to your god—
they simply just said no."

The king being full of fury,
said make the furnace hot.
Make it seven times the usual heat—
so hot, it'll spare them not.

(Dan. 3)

A Second Dream

The king had a second dream,
which Daniel interpreted as—
the king would be driven out from
Men, and he would eat grass.

"You shall dwell in the fields
with the beast of the field.
You shall be wet with the dew of

heaven, for God gives to whom He will.

"Your hair will grow long as eagle's feathers.
You will grow nails like a bird's claw.
He must have been something to see,
because this is what man saw—

"Seven times shall pass over you,
until you know the most high's rule."
All these things came to pass,
because Daniel's interpretations were cool.

The king blessed the Lord on high,
and his reason returned to him.
He was established back into his kingdom.
God's rules; He would follow them.

Now I, Nebuchadnezzer praised and extol and
honor the King of Heaven, all whose work
are truth and His ways judgment:...
(Dan. 4:37)

The Writing on the Wall

King Belshazzar, Nebuchadnezzar's son,
saw God's writing on the wall.
He called for his wise men to interpret,
but they could not understand at all.

Now, his queen told him she knew of a
man named Daniel, "Whom your father used;
he is able to show the meaning.
He will tell you the real news."

He offered Daniel gifts of gold if

he could make him understand.
Daniel told him to keep his gifts, for
Daniel worked for the main man.

Daniel's interpretations of the writing,
well, what he said came true.
The king was slain in the night; then
Darius took his kingdom too.

Darius set Daniel over princes and
presidents, of whom Daniel came first.
Daniel's spirit was of excellence, which made
them look the worst.

*And over these three, presidents; of whom Daniel was
first the princes might give account unto them...*
(Dan. 6:1)

Daniel

Daniel was a prophet
taken from his land
along with Shadrach, Meshach, and Abed-Nego—
three wise and gifted men.

Although God always came first,
Daniel then served the king.
Daniel, through God's guidance,
could interpret the king's dreams.

Now, look out Daniel, here come
some men, and they're full of sin.
They're going to get you thrown
into the lion's den.

But don't you worry, and don't you fret.
Your trust is in the Lord;
He'll keep the lion's mouth shut.
God will send an angel to stand guard.

He's the living God and steadfast forever.
He works His wonders and His miracles.
He helps us to endeavor.

So Daniel prospered and lived a long life
of prophecy and warning through his dreams at night.

So Daniel prospered in the reign of Darius
and in the reign of Cyrus the Persian
(Dan. 6:28).

Daniel's Dream

Daniel had a dream, which
was more like a vision.
He wrote it down at once—
the minute he had arisen.

It told of four great beasts—
each different from another—
one like a lion, a bear, a leopard,
and one much scarier than the others.

For it had horns plucked by the roots,
and a little horn with man's eyes,
and a mouth speaking of great things,
and how that voice did rise.

Daniel grieved in his spirit and his body,
for the vision troubled him.
When he asked them what they meant,
God then interpreted them—

"These four great beasts are four kings,
which shall arise out of the earth.
The saints of the Most High shall
take and possess forever My turf."

(Dan. 7)

*But go thou way till the end be: for thou shall rest and
stand in thy lot at the end of the days.*
(Dan. 12:13)

HOSEA

Hosea's Family

The Lord sent Hosea to get a wife.
She came from among the harlots.
He married Gomer; they had children;
but she couldn't forget where she started.

Their firstborn was a boy named by God.
Jezreel he was called.
Then came a girl named Loruhamah, for
God would have no mercy at all.

When Gomer weaned her daughter,
another son was conceived.
God said he would not be there or
supply them with what they would need.

But when the many children of Judah and
Israel shall gather and appoint one head,
they shall then come up out of the land—
a great day of Jezreel, is what God said.

(Hosea 1 and 2)

... And the Lord said to Hosea, go, take unto thee a wife of whoredoms, and children of whoredoms; for the land hath committed great whoredom departing from the Lord. (....)

Hosea's Unfaithful Wife

Plead with your mother, children,
for she is not my wife;
neither am I her husband, until
she put away her whoredom life.

For your mother has played the harlot;
she that conceived has lived in shame.
She takes all that she has to her lovers,
and they show her their disdain.

She will chase them, but will not catch
them, for them she will not find.
She will seek then her first husband,
for it was better for her at that time.

I will then destroy her vines and fig trees,
for they were her lovers' rewards.
I will take away the names of the idols,
and their memories I will retard.

I will even betroth thee unto me in faithfulness;
and thou shall know the Lord
(Hosea 2:20)

Israel—The Harlot

God compared His people
to the harlot of the night—
they behaved shamefully
and never seemed to get it right.

"They turn their backs on the one who
feeds them. They give away My stuff to Baal.
I will destroy all My rewards I've given you.
You don't deserve them at all.

"There shall come a day, I will betroth
you to Me. It will be forever.
Yes, I will betroth you in all righteousness.
Those who are not my people shall gather.

"I will say to them, 'Thou art My people,'
and they will call Me their God.
I will show mercy to those of you
that has given Me the nod."

There is truth, mercy, or knowledge
shown by God in the land.
Your many sins overtake the good. You'll
be destroyed, because you don't understand.

(Hosea 2 and 3)

Come Home, Backslider

Backslider, return to the Lord your God.
It's time to return, come home.
Sin has caused you to stumble.
In Christ is where you belong.

Ask the Lord to take away your
iniquities and receive you with grace.
Ask God to show you mercy.
It's time to get back into the race.

God will heal your backsliding.
His love for you is free.
He turned His back in anger.
Now grow as the beautiful lily.

Those that return will grow like a
vine, and their scent will be as wine.
The ways of the Lord are right.
Let God deliver you from that bind.

Walk in the ways of our Lord.
I tell you His ways are right.
He'll pick you up when you stumble;
help you walk in His righteous light.

(Hosea 14:1-9)

JOEL

Joel—The Prophet

Hear this, people; listen, and tell
your children just what you hear.
The worms and locust have ravished
the land; nothing is still left here.

Awake, you drunkards, and weep,
all you drinkers of wine.
All new wine is taken away.
It's time to hear you whine.

Be ashamed, all you vinedressers.
Howl loudly and be ashamed.
Your wine has dried up, your trees withered,
and the joys of man are tame.

Sanctify yourself a fast; gather all
the inhabitants of the land.
Call the elders together, for
the day of the Lord is at hand.

Repent, repent, repent,
for the day of the Lord is at hand!

*Alas, for the day! For the day of the Lord is at hand,
and as a destruction from the Almighty shall it come*
(Joel 1:15)

God's Wonders

God will cause the rain to come down.
Rejoice for the latter rain.
The threshing floors shall be full of wheat.
God will take away the pain.

He will restore to you the years
that the locust has eaten.
He will send His great army among you.
Praise God, for you are not beaten.

He is the Lord your God,
and there is no other.
You shall not be put to shame,
for His Spirit is in you, brother.

Your sons and daughters shall prophesy.
Your old men shall dream.
Your young men shall see visions.
God will show us what it all means.

God will show us wonders in heaven,
and in the earth, blood, fire, and pillars of smoke.
Before the terrible day of the Lord,
comes God's power, and it's no joke.

The sun shall be turned into darkness,
and the moon into blood.
Before the terrible day of the Lord come
as the day of the flood.

(Joel 2)

... whosoever shall call on the Name of
the Lord, shall be delivered...
(Joel 2:32)

Merlene Tarver Howard

The Day of the Lord

Blow the trumpet in Zion;
then sound an alarm.
Let the inhabitants of the land tremble.
A day of darkness and gloom threatens harm.

This is the day of the Lord—it has
come and it is at hand.
There has never been another like this,
and it is spread across the land.

The land before you is as the garden
of Eden and a desolate wilderness behind.
Nothing shall escape them, and
their destruction will not be kind.

The earth shall shake before them.
They will make the heavens tremble.
The sun, the moon, the stars shall be dark.
They shall move fast and shall be nimble.

The Lord shall utter His voice before
His army for His camp is very great.
His day will be terrible, and
there will be no escape.

And it shall come to pass, that whosoever shall call
on the name of the Lord shall be delivered...
(Joel 2:32)

AMOS

Amos

The words of Amos, who
was a farmer, were thus—
"The Lord will roar from Zion,
and utter a word for us."

Thus said the Lord—"For three transgressions
of Damascus and for four,
I will not turn away punishment,
so listen to me, there is more.

"To the house of Hazael, I will send
a fire to devour Benhadad.
I will break the bar of Damascus;
cut them off for being bad.

"Syria, Gaza, Ashdod, Tyrus
shall all feel My wrath.
I will not turn away their punishment,
for they have walked the wrong path."

These are some of the cities—
just to name a few.
God will punish many more,
their kings, and their princes too.

And their Kings shall go into captivity,
he and his Princes together, said the Lord
(Amos 1:15)

Hear Ye this Word

You shall not drink from your vineyards;
you shall not drink the wine.
Therefore the prudent shall keep quiet,
for it is an evil time.

God knows your manifold transgressions
and your mighty sins.
You turn away your poor at the gates,
for surely you are ungodly men.

Hate the evil, and love the good.
Establish judgment at the gate.
It may be that the Lord God of Host
will be gracious, so just you wait.

In all vineyards, there will be wailing;
wailing shall be in the streets,
for the day of the Lord shall be darkness—
all light indeed shall flee.

God will not accept your offerings,
neither burnt nor offerings of meat,
neither peace offerings that you offer,
offerings of your fat beasts.

Take away your noisy songs—
He will not hear their melody.
He will cause you to become captives.
Woe to those who do not see.

(Amos 5)

Amos Prophesied

Amos prophesied—"Jeroboam shall die by the sword.
Then Israel shall be led away captive."
Then Amaziah warned Amos to flee to
another land, for you to inhabit.

Amos said, "I was not a prophet,
but a breeder of sheep.
God sent me to prophesy to his people,
to put His Word in the street.

"Thy sons and thy daughters shall fall
by the sword, and thy wife shall be the whore.
God will put an end to His people.
He will not pass by them anymore.

"This the Lord has shown me, and
behold, a basket of summer fruit.
He said, 'The end has come to My Israelite people.
There is nothing more they can do.'"

Shall not the land tremble for this?
Everyone who lives there shall mourn.
God will cause the sun to go down at noon,
and the darkness will be in the morn.

All the sinners of God's people shall
die by the sword that say evil will not overtake us.
God will rebuild His cities, and His people
shall inhabit them, certainly not the unjust.

*And I will plant them upon the land, and they shall no more
be pulled up out of their land... saith the Lord thy God.*
(Amos 9:15)

OBADIAH

The Vision of Obadiah

Thus said the Lord concerning Edom—
"I have made you small among the heathen.
Thou are greatly despised.
The pride of your heart has deceived you—
pride has left you unwise.

"Your friends shall force you out—
those that eat your bread.
You shouldn't look on the day of their calamity,
for your reward is on your own head.

For the day of the Lord is near.
What you have done will be done to you.
Upon Mount Zion shall be deliverance.
The house of Esau shall be destroyed too.

And saviors shall come up on Mount Zion
to judge the mountains of Esau.
The kingdom shall be the Lord's—
that is what Obadiah saw.

(Obad. 1:21)

JONAH

Jonah's Lesson

"Arise, go to Nineveh," the Lord told Jonah,
but Jonah, he wouldn't go.
"You'll just forgive them of their wickedness,
this I do know.

"I'll flee to Taishish from God's presence."
He found a ship and paid his fare.
Down he went into its bottom,
like God couldn't find him there.

A storm rose up and scared the captain,
and they cast a lot on him.
They then threw him into the sea.
Jonah, I hope you can swim.

The Lord prepared a great fish to swallow Jonah.
Three days in his belly he did sit.
Jonah prayed, and he repented;
so God made the big fish spit.

Back on land, he preached at Nineveh;
said what God told him to say.
Then the Lord blessed the people,
for it had to be God's way.

"Lord, I know you are forgiving, merciful,
slow to anger, one who relents from doing harm.
It makes me so very angry,
now I wish I'd never been born."

God used a plant to teach Jonah
of His mercy and to show His great will.
Jonah sure learned his lesson
of God's peace; be still.

When my soul fainted within me I remembered the Lord:
and my prayer came in unto thee, into thine holy temple.
(Jon. 2:7)

MICAH

The Wicked Rules

Hear, O house of Israel, is it not for
you to know judgment,.
who hates the good and loves the evil,
those who eat the flesh of those God sent.

You break the bones of my people,
then chop them into little pieces.
When they cry to the Lord, he will not hear,
for you listen to what false prophets teach.

Truly I am full of power, by the Spirit of the Lord
and of judgment and might,
to declare unto Jacob his transgressions,
and to tell Israel to get it right.

The leaders judge for rewards,
and the priests, they work for pay.
The prophets they divine for money,
when they know this is not God's way.

Therefore shall Zion be plowed as a field,
and Jerusalem shall become a heap.
This is done for your sake,
for what you have done to His sheep.

Therefore shall Zion for your sake,
be plowed as a field...
(Mic. 3:12)

The Joy of Restoration

In the last days, it shall come to pass that
the house of the Lord shall be established
on the mountain top.
Many nations shall come to the Lord's mountain,
where His Word has never stopped.

He shall judge among many people,
and rebuke strong nations far off.
They shall turn swords into plows and
spears into pruning hook, as their hearts turn soft.

There will be no further need for war,
as man sit under his shade tree.
The mouth of God has spoken,
so that is the way it shall be.

Arise and thresh, O daughter of Zion.
I will make your horns iron and hoof brass.
You should beat into pieces many people.
God shall make these things come to pass.

(Mic. 4)

*And he shall stand and feed in the strength of the Lord,
in the majesty of the name of the Lord his God; and they
shall abide: for now shall be great unto the ends of the earth*
(Mic. 5:4)

Woe is Me!

Woe is me! The good man is perished
out of the earth; there is none upright.
They do evil and wait for a reward.
Trust none; your own family is not right.

The sons dishonor the father; the
daughter rises against mother.
A man's house is full of enemies;
can't even trust his own brother.

Therefore I will look unto the Lord.
I will wait until God hears me.
God will be my light unto me,
for His light shines for all to see.

I shall behold His righteousness.
I shall feed your people with your rod.
He will have compassion upon us.
We shall fear our Lord, our God.

Thou will perform the truth of Jacob
and the mercy to Abraham,
which you have sworn to our fathers.
When He subdues our sins, we will be gentle as lambs.

(Mic. 7)

Rejoice not against me O mine enemy:
when I fall, I shall arise; when I sit in darkness,
the Lord shall be a light unto me.
(Mic. 7:8)

NAHUM

Nahum's Vision

God is jealous, and the Lord
reserve wrath for His enemies,
although slow to anger and great
in power is the vision Nahum sees.

The Lord has His way in the whirlwind.
The clouds are dust off His feet.
He dries up the rivers, and
He rebukes the mighty seas.

The mountains quake at Him;
the hills can only melt.
The earth burns at His presence;
to the world His might is felt.

Who can stand before His indignation?
Who can live in His fury?
Rocks better move out of His way,
and evil had better hurry.

The Lord is good—a stronghold
in the time of trouble.
He knows them that trust in Him,
while evil will be devoured as dry stubble.

(Nah. 1)

... O Judah, keep thy solemn feasts, perform thy vows: for the
wicked shall no more pass through thee; he is utterly cut off
(Nah. 1:15)

HABAKKUK

The Chaldean's Rule

The burden which Habakkuk,
the prophet, did see—
"O Lord, how long shall I cry and thou
will not hear me?

"I even cry out to you of violence,
and you will not save.
Violence and strife are before me.
Behold, I will work in your ways.

"I will work a work in your days,
which you will not believe.
Although it will be told to you,
you still will not receive.

"The terrible and the dreadful, their judgment
and their dignity proceed them.
They shall come all for violence.
O Holy God, leave us not out on a limb.

"Thou has ordained them for judgment,
and established them for correction.
Thou are purer eyes than behold evil.
The righteous man needs your protection.

"Shall they continue to slay the nation
and show us no pity?
Burn their incense to their god
and their portions remain plenty?"

(Hab. 1)

I will stand upon my watch, and set me upon the
tower, and will watch to see what He will say unto
me, and what I shall answer when I am reproved.
(Hab. 2:1)

Habakkuk's Prayer

O Lord, I heard Thy speech and was afraid.
Revive Thy works in the midst of the years.
In Thy wrath, remember mercy.
O Lord, thy speech I do hear.

God's glory covers the heaven;
the earth was full of His praise.
His brightness was as the light;
the mountains tremble at His ways.

You went forth for the salvation of

your people, even for your anointed.
When I heard You, my belly trembled;
rot entered my bones, as they were unjointed.

Although the fig tree will not blossom,
neither shall fruit be on the vine,
yet I will rejoice in thee, O Lord.
Joy and salvation shall be mine.

The Lord God is my strength...
(Hab. 3:19)

ZEPHANIAH

Zephaniah's Warning

The prophecy of Zephaniah told of God's
judgments—some at a time to come.
The day of the Lord will bring purpose both
to mankind and earth; God's will will be done.

The Word of the Lord came to Zephaniah—
"I will consume all things off the land.
I will consume beast, fowl, and fish.
I will cut off the land from man."

Hold thy peace at the presence of God,
for the day of the Lord is at hand.
He has prepared a sacrifice for His guest.
The remnants of Baal can't stand.

The great day of the Lord is near.
That day is a day of wrath;
a day of darkness, gloom, and distress.
Nothing can stand in His path.

Distress shall fall on men; they will
walk as if they were blind.
Neither gold nor silver shall deliver them.
Because of sin God's wrath is on time.

(Zeph. 1)

*I will utterly consume all things from
off the land, saith the Lord.*
(Zeph. 1:2)

God is in the Midst

Woe to her that is filthy and polluted;
to the oppressing city.
She disobeyed the voice, received no correction,
and drew not to God; what a pity!

God fails not, and the just God is in the midst;
every morning he bring judgment.
There is no shame in Him that do not fail.
He cuts off all nations; no man is left to inhabit.

Then He will turn to the people a pure language,
that they may all call His name.
To serve Him as one, sing, O daughter of Zion,
rejoice, for in our hearts we are all the same.

The Lord has taken away our judgment.
Thou shall see evil no more.
God is in the midst; He will save.
He will rejoice over us with joy evermore.

He will sing; behold, He will heal the sick.
He will gather together those driven out.
He will give us praise and fame.
Those put to shame will have clout.

Sing, O daughter of Zion; shout, O Israel; be glad and
rejoice with all the heart, O daughter of Jerusalem.
(Zeph. 3:14)

HAGGAI

It is Time
The Book of Haggai

Thus said the Lord of Host, saying,
"The people say, the time has not come—
the time that the Lord's house should be built.
The people said it could not be done."

The Lord said, "Consider your ways.
You have sown much and got back a little bit.
You eat but can't get enough; your small
wages seem to go into a bottomless pit.

"Go to the mountain and bring wood.
Build the house, and I will take pleasure inside.
In there," said the Lord of Host,
"I will also be glorified.

"You run to your houses, while Mine lay
in waste—each man to his own.
I will call for a drought upon the land.
There shall be waste to everyone's homes."

There was those that obeyed the voice of God.
They listened to Haggai, the prophet's, words.
The Lord stirred up their spirits. The remnants of people,
on God's house they then worked.

(Hag. 1)

It is time for you O ye to dwell in your ceiled
houses, and this house lie waste? (....)

Haggai Speaks Again

"Be strong, O Zerubbabel, and Joshua, be strong.
All ye people of the land and work,
I am with you as I was in Egypt.
Fear not, for in a little while I will shake the earth.

"I will shake the heavens and the sea.
I will shake all the nations too.
I will fill this house with glory.
It will stir up the spirit in you.

"The glory of this latter house shall be greater
than the former," said the Lord of Host,
"In this place I will give My peace,
as I fill this house the most."

Again God's Word came to Haggai—
He that touches you, touches the apple of His eye.
He will shake His hand upon them,
and you shall know the reason why.

Speak to Zerubbabel, governor of Judah saying,
I will shake the heavens and the earth; and I
will overthrow the throne of kingdoms...
(Hag. 2:21-22)

(Hag. 2)

ZECHARIAH

Thus Said the Lord of Host

O Lord of Host, how long will you not have
mercy on your children and their cities.
You have had anger all these years.
The angel of the Lord ask for your pity.

The Lord answered the angel with
good and comfortable words.
And the angel said unto me, "The Lord
is jealous and very displeased, ye earth.

"Therefore said the Lord, 'I am returning
to Jerusalem with my mercies.
My house shall be built in it.
I was but a little displeased.

"'Cry out saying thus,' said the Lord
of Host, 'my cities through prosperity shall be
spread abroad, yet I comfort Zion, and
yet choose Jerusalem. Lift your eyes and see.'

"I lifted my eyes and saw, and behold,
four horns. I asked, 'What be these?'
He answered, 'These are the four horns which
scattered My people with whom I am not pleased.'

Then He showed me four carpenters.
I asked, 'What does these come to do?'
'They have come to scatter the horns—
cast them out for all of you.'"

(Zech. 1)

Then lifted I up mine eyes, and saw,
and behold four horns
(Zech. 1:18)

When Zechariah Asked

When Zechariah asked, "O my Lord,
what are these?" an angel said to me,
"I will show you just what these be."

The man under the myrtle trees answered
and said, "These are sent by the Lord
to walk to and fro through the land,
looking in every field and every yard."

The angel of the Lord said, "We have walked
to and fro through the earth, and behold,
all the earth sits still and is at rest.
How long will thou not let mercy roll?"

Behold, the angel that talked with me went
forth, and another angel went out to meet him;
said unto him, "Run. Speak to this young man o
Jerusalem's inhabitance—the multitude of them.

"For said the Lord, 'I will be a wall of fire
round about and be glory in the midst.
Deliver thyself, O Zion, that dwell with the
daughter of Babylon, dwell in joy and bliss.'"

Sing and rejoice O daughter of Zion: for lo I
come and I will dwell in the midst of thee…
(Zech. 2:10)

MALACHI

Malachi

The burden of the word of the Lord to Israel by Malachi
(Mal. 1:1)

"I have loved you," said the Lord,
Yet you ask Me in what way?
Was Esau not Jacob's brother?
I loved Jacob, hated Esau, whom I made pay.

I have hated Esau and laid waste to his
Heritage. What they build, I will tear down.
They shall be called wicked people.
I will have indignation for their towns.

A son honors his father and servant, his master.
If I am your Father, where is My fear?
You say you have despised My name,
Polluted My altars, offered Me foul ears.

You expect Me to except your blind, lame,
And sick sacrifices. Is it not evil?
Offer them to your Governor.
He too will fine them feeble

... I have no pleasure in you saith the Lord of Host...
(Mal. 1:10)

Will Man Rob God

Will a man rob God? Yet ye have robbed Me.
Where have you robbed Me?
In tithes and offerings, you are cursed with
A curse the whole nation will see.

Bring all the tithes into the storehouse
That there be meat in Mine house
"Prove me now," said the Lord of Host, "and I will
Open a window of heaven and pour blessings out."

"All nations shall call you blessed for you shall
Be a delightsome land," said the Lord of Host.

Those that heard my book and listened and
Feared the name of the Lord the most,

They shall be mine in the day when I
Make up my jewels. I will spare them
As a man spares his own son that serves him.
I will discern between good and evil's rim.

For I am the Lord, I change not; therefore,
You sons of Jacob are not consumed.
Return unto Me, and I will return unto you.
If not than you will be doomed.

(Mal. 3)

*And He shall turn the hearts of the fathers to the
children, and the hearts of the children to their fathers,
lest I come and smite the earth with a curse.*
(Mal. 3:6)

NEW TESTAMENT

MATHEW

Matthew

From Abraham to Jesus
From Abraham to David, there were fourteen
Generations, from David to Babylon fourteen more,
From Babylon to Christ, fourteen generations.
God sent His Son to open the door.

Now the birth of Christ was a holy birth.
His mother Mary knew no man.
Joseph, her betrothed a just man, God
Appeared in a dream to make him understand.

Behold, a virgin, until her firstborn,
She gave birth to Jesus our Lord.
Both Joseph and Mary obeyed the Father
And lived a Holy Ghost life from the start.

They followed the angel's advice and knew
Not each other until after the blessed birth.
They then made love, had kids of their own,
And loved them for all that it's worth.

And knew her not till she brought forth her
firstborn son: and called his name Jesus
(Matt. 1:25)

Jesus was Born

Now Jesus was born in Bethlehem
In the days of Herod the king.
There came wise men from the east
Following the bright star they had seen.

We came from afar to worship
The new King of the Jews.
This troubled King Herod very much.
Jesus, I won't share my reign with you.

He gathered all the chief priest and
Scribes, and this he demanded of them.
Where is the Christ Child, born to the
Jews? I really must find Him.

Then Herod asked the wise men
Where they saw the star appear?
Go find the Child and bring me word.
Just bring the way back here.

The wise men followed the star; it
Led them to the Christ Child that day.
While Herod waited for their return
They left, but went another way.

(Matt. 2:1-12)

... they departed into their own country another way.
(Matt. 2:12)

The Nazarene

The wise men didn't tell Herod
Where the Christ child was.
An angel brought Joseph a message,
And it came from God above.

You must take your family, and
Into Egypt you must flee.
For Herod seek to find Him
To do a nasty, deadly deed.

He is killing all the male children,
So depart until he is dead.
You can then return to Israel
Is what the angel said.

Joseph took his family, and
They made a quick get away.
The angel said, "Don't fret
For you can return some day."

After Heron died, it was safe
For them to return back home.
They lived in a town called Nazareth,
So the "Nazarene" was how Jesus was known.

And He came and dwelt in a city called Nazareth...
He shall be called a Nazarene
(Matt. 2:23)

Merlene Tarver Howard

The Temptation of Jesus

Jesus fasted for forty days and nights;
Afterward, He was hungry.
That's when the devil came to Him.
Jesus showed him how it would be.

Devil: If thou be hungry then,
Turn these stones into bread.
Jesus: Man does not live by bread alone,
But by the word of God instead.

The devil; took Him to the temple top
Said; Son of God cast your self down.
You will not be hurt for
The angels are all around.

Jesus: thou shall not tempt the Lord thy God
For it is written again.
Satan couldn't make Him do anything
For he is not like mortal men.

The devil then took Him, to a high mountain,
Where He could see the world.
Said "You can have all of this
If You give me a whirl."

Jesus answered saying, "Get thee behind me Satan;
It is written that you shall serve Me."
The devil left defeated, for
That's the way it will always be.

Then the devil leaveth him, and behold
angels came and ministered unto him
(Matt. 4:11)

306

The Beatitudes

And He opened his mouth and taught them saying,
(Matt. 5:2)

Blessed are the poor in Spirit, for
You shall inherit heaven's Kingdom.
Blessed are those who moan,
You will be comforted in His home.

Blessed are the meek,
You shall inherit the Earth.
Being meek and humble, God will
Show you what you are worth.

Blessed are those that are hungry
And thirst for righteousness.
You shall be filled, just remember,
God has promised you this.

Blessed are the merciful; you
Shall obtain mercy, new mercies every day.
His mercy is in abundant;
It is in your hearts, and it will stay.

Blessed be the pure in heart,
You shall see God's face.
Isn't that enough to keep you
Running in this race?

Blessed are the peacemaker,
For God's children you are called.
We are a special people,
And we can have it all.

Blessed are the persecuted for Righteousness sake,
For yours is the kingdom of Heaven.
Although, they persecute you,
You must forgive them seven times seven.

Blessed are you that are reviled, and
All evil is against you for His sake.
Rejoice and be glad, for great is
His reward when you enter at the gate.

Rejoice and be exceeding glad: for great is
your reward in heaven: for so persecuted they
the prophets which were before you
(Matt. 5:12)

(Matt. 5:3-12)

Be Blessed His Twelve

And when He had called unto Him, His
Twelve disciples, He gave them power,
Power against the unclean spirits, to cast them
Out, heal the sick, and to go forth at any hour.

Now the names of the twelve apostles are
These, Simon called Peter, and Andrew his brother,
James, son of Zebedee, his brother John, Philip
And Bartholomew, Thomas, and Matthew, and others.

James son of Alphaeus, and Lebbaeus whose
Surname was Thaddaeus, Simon the Canaanite
Judas Iscariot, who betrayed Him
These are the twelve sent forth by Christ.

Go ye preach, saying the kingdom is at hand.
Heal the sick, raise the dead.
Cast out devil, give freely as you receive, provide
Not gold or silver in your purse, but be worthy instead.

(Matt. 10)

Behold I send you forth as sheep in the midst of wolves...
(Matt. 10:16)

A Sea Walk

In the fourth watch of the night,
Jesus came to them walking on the sea.
When the disciples saw they were troubled,
And wondered how this could be.

It is a spirit they cried out.
Their cries were cries of fear.
Jesus said, "It is I, be not afraid.
Be of good cheer."

Peter said, "Lord, if it be Thou,
Bid me to come to Thee."
Jesus said, "Come" and Peter did.
He also walked on the sea.

But when he saw the boisterous
Winds, he was just plain afraid.
He begun to sink at once.
"Save me" is what he said.

Immediately, Jesus stretched forth
His hands and caught him as he cried out.
"O thou of little faith," said Christ,
"Wherefore did thou doubt?"

(Matt. 14:25-31)

He Arose

The angel sent the women, not one but a few
To tell the disciples, what they already knew.
Jesus had informed them, of how He would arise.
He told them of this wondrous thing
while He walked by their sides.
To die on the cross that day was His plan.
To be buried, rise again, and ascend from this land.
The men, His disciples, ran to the tomb to peep.
Found Jesus had arose, this One that they did seek.
He appeared before others, that faithful day.
Now we have the message He has shown us the way.
He arose, He has arisen, now He is home!

(Matt. 28)

MARK

Following Jesus

Now as He walked by the sea of Galilee,
He saw Simon and Andrew his brother.
They were casting a net into the sea
For they were fishermen and none other.

Jesus said to them, "Come with Me;
I will make you fishers of men."
They dropped their nets and followed
Him; their discipleship had began.

As He went a little farther, He saw James
And John, brothers mending nets.
He called them; they answered Him.
But they haven't seen any thing yet.

He went into the synagogue on the Sabbath
Where He taught His doctrine.
There was a man, who had a spirit,
But the spirit was unclean.

Jesus rebuked him saying, "Hold thy peace,
And come out of him."
The unclean spirit, with a loud voice, came out.
Immediately the word spread; He amazed all of them.

(Mark 1)

And straightway they forsook their nets and followed Him
(Mark 1:18)

I'm Sure He's the One

Where did this man come from?
Is he not the carpenter's son?
Is his mother not called Mary?
I'm pretty sure, He's the one.

But how did he get such knowledge,
Mighty works, and wisdom too?
Now how can we believe him,
When we've known him from His youth?

Their criticism and their mocking
Made Jesus have to leave.
He couldn't perform his works there
Because of negativity and unbelief.

Is He not the Son of God,
Sent here and was made flesh?
To die for all us sinners
Who gave Him no respect?

He was called Jesus the Christ;
I believe that he is the one.
There is no doubt God sent Him,
His only begotten Son.

(Mark 6)

*But Jesus said unto them, a prophet is not
without honour, but in his own country, and
among his kin, and in his own house.*
(Mark 6:4)

The Death of John, the Baptist

When Herod heard of Jesus,
This is what he thought:
John whom I had beheaded, has arisen,
And now this dead man walks.

You see he had sent John to prison
Because of what he had said.
You and your wife are sinners,
Then his wife wanted John dead.

Herod feared John because he was a
Holy man who spoke out and it was true.
His wife's daughter's dance pleased him
Said he, "I'll give anything to you."

She asked for John, the Baptist's head
On a platter and would have nothing less.
His head became her gift, to her mother,
While his disciple buried the rest.

... and gave it to the damsel; and the
damsel gave it to her mother
(Mark 6:28)

... they came and took up his corpse and laid it in a tomb
(Mark 6:29)

Merlene Tarver Howard

He Does All Things Well

He does all things well. He makes the deaf to hear,
And the dumb to speak,
The multitude who was hungry,
He gave them food to eat.

But having eyes, you still can't see.
Having ears, you hear not.
Can't you remember the multitude I fed?
From a few fish I fed the lot.

He took the blind man by the hand,
Spit, and opened his eyes to see.
He sent him away, don't go into town,
Or tell anyone about me.

He taught His disciples of how he'd be killed,
And on the third day rise again.
Peter get thee behind, for you savior things
Not of God, but things that be of men.

Be not ashamed, take up your cross, and follow
The Lord; give up your silver and gold
For what shall it profit, to gain the whole
World if you should lose your own soul?

(Mark 7:37, Mark 8)

The Signs?

Peter, James, and John asked Jesus, tell us
The signs when will these things be?
Jesus answered them to take heed,
For they asked Him in privacy.

Jesus said, "Take heed that no one deceives
You, for many will come in My name."
Saying I am He and will deceive many people of God.
I want you to know this is not My aim.

When you hear of wars and rumors of wars,
Be not troubled, for it is not time yet.
For nation will be against nation and
In various places, there shall be earthquakes.

There will be famines and troubles,
Know these are the beginning of sorrow.
Beware, watch out for yourselves,
Be prepared for what may come tomorrow.

(Mark 13)

Go Ye Into All the World

Go ye into all the world to preach
The gospel to every creature.
He that believes shall be baptized;
Then he too can become a preacher.

He that believes not shall be damned.
He that believes shall cast devils out.
They shall speak in new tongues,
And follow Me without doubts.

They shall take up serpents and if they
Drink any deadly thing, it won't hurt them.
They shall lay hands on the sick, they shall
Recover, though their lives may look dim.

After the Lord had spoken to them,
He was received into heaven by God's side.
They went forth in Jesus's name
Preaching the word and with signs.

(Mark 16:15-20)

And they went forth and preached... and confirming
the word with signs following, Amen
(Mark 16:20)

LUKE

Jesus at Twelve

When Jesus was only twelve years old,
His family went to Jerusalem for the feast.
Afterward, they started home, Jesus stayed behind.
They of course had to return, for Jesus they did seek.

After three days, they found the child in the temple, with
Doctors, both hearing and asking of them.
When they saw him, they were amazed at the
Understand and knowledge of him.

Why is it that you seek me? He asked I must
Get about the business of My Father, now.
But he went home with his parents to Nazareth;
His wisdom and stature only grew and wow.

His parents didn't understand what he spoke;
To them, but Mary kept these in her heart.
Jesus grew in favor with God and man.
Yes, indeed, He was real smart.

(Luke 2)

And Jesus increased in wisdom and stature,
and in favor with God and man
(Luke 2:52)

Preaching in the Wilderness

The Word of the Lord came unto John
Son of Zacharias, in the wilderness.
He was preaching the baptism, and
Repentance of sins, to all who would hear this.

He was the voice of one crying,
"Prepare ye the way of the Lord."
"All flesh shall see the salvation, of God
O, you vipers, be on guard."

When asked if he was the Christ,
He answered unto them all.
I, indeed, baptize you with water, while
The one that comes after me stands tall.

I am not worthy to unloose His shoe;
He will baptize you with Holy Ghost fire.
He preached this and many other things.
He will be worthy to be called sire.

(Luke 3)

And many other things in his exhortation
preached he unto the people
(Luke 3:18)

Rebuking Devils and Diseases

In the synagogue, there was a man.
Who had a spirit of an unclean devil.
He cried out with a loud voice:
"Leave us alone, Jesus, let us stay and revel."

We know who You are; we know
You are of God, and the Holy One.
Jesus rebuked them saying, "Hold thy peace,
Come out, your work in him is done."

When the devil was thrown in the midst,
He came out and hurt him not.
They were amazed at the power
And the authority that Jesus's word got.

He left the synagogue, went to Simon's house
Where Simon's mother-in-law had a fever.
He rebuked that fever and immediately
She arose for the fever did leave her.

As the sun was setting, many sick came
With diver's diseases and everyone was healed.
Devils came out of many; Jesus the
Son of God was truly revealed.

And the devils also came out of many crying
out... and He rebuking them suffered them not
to speak: for they knew that He was Christ
(Luke 4:41)

Follow Me

Jesus taught the people from
Simon the fisherman's boat.
Afterward he told Simon to let
Down his nets, he answered and I quote.

"Master, we have toiled all night and have taken in nothing,
But at thy word we will let down the net."
And when he had done so, there were so many
Fish; they even shared their catch.

Simon Peter saw all this and fell
Down at the Savior's feet.
"Come and follow Me, I will make you
Fishers of all the men you meet."

Then He saw Levi, and said unto
Him: "Come, follow Me."
Levi made a feast that day; Jesus
Ate with the publicans, Why? Said the Pharisees.

When you are well, you need not a doctor,
But the sick most certainly do.
I came not to call the righteous but
Sinners, does that not answer you?

I came not to call the righteous, but sinners to repentance.
(Luke 5:32)

The Alabaster Box

And behold a woman in the city,
Which was a sinner.
She brought an alabaster box
Of ointment when she entered.

She stood at His feet, and she was weeping.
She began to wipe His feet.
She used her tears, to wash and her hair to dry.
With her ointment she made them smell sweet.

The Pharisee's saw this and spoke, saying,
"What kind of woman do you let touch?"
If you were a prophet, you would
Not let her touch you so much.

Jesus said, "If two people owed you money,
One five hundred, and only fifty the other,
You forgive them both, who will love you most,
Less or more, my brother?"

You gave no water; she gave me her tears,
Which she dried with her hair.
You gave me no kiss, but she has kissed my feet
While down there.

And He said unto her, Thy sins are forgiven
(Luke 7:48)

Merlene Tarver Howard

The Prodigal Son

A certain man had two sons; the younger of

Them asked for his portion of goods.
His father divided and gave to him his;
He took off to a far place as fast as he could.

There arose a famine in the land;
He had partied and wasted all he had.
He went to a citizen of the country who
Gave him the swine to feed, better call your dad.

He filled his belly with the pig's husks,
And no man gave anything to him.
He thought the servant of my father's house
Ate better, for my father took care of them.

So he went back home, and while he was a long ways off,
His father ran and kissed him on the neck.
He said, "Father, I am a sinner,
Not worthy to be treated as a pet."

But his father put on him a robe and shoes,
And on his hand a ring.
Kill the fatted calf and be merry.
We will celebrate today this thing.

My son was dead but is alive again.
The lost is now the found.
Play music, dance, and be happy.
Let's make a joyful sound.

(Luke 15)

The Lost is Found

Now his older brother was in the field
And heard the music and the dancing.
He called one of the servants to ask him
What was going on, and why were they all laughing.

The servant replied, "Thy brother is back,
And your father has killed the fatted calf."
This really made him mad, Why?
I stayed home while he spent his half.

He refused to go in, so his father
Came out and said, "Son, won't you come in?"
He answered saying, "I have stayed home,
And there's no telling where he has been."

I served you all this time, and
I obeyed your every command.
You've never given me a feast,
Yet you celebrate this sinner man.

Son, you are ever with me and
All I have is also thine.
Your brother who was dead now
Lives again; we should be merry at this time.

... for this thy brother was dead, and is alive
again and was lost, and is found.
(Luke 15:32)

Saying Good-bye

As they spoke, Jesus stood before them
said unto them, "Peace be with you."

But they were terrified and afraid.
They didn't know what to do.

Jesus said to them, "Why are you troubled?
Why in your hearts, are your thoughts so wrong?
Behold my feet and my hands. I am
Not a spirit; I have flesh and bones."

And when He had spoken, He
Showed them His hands and His feet.
While they believed not for joy,
He asked them, "Have ye here any meat?"

They gave to Him a piece of honeycomb,
And a piece of broiled fish, you see
All things must be fulfilled, which were
Written in the law concerning Me.

You are witnesses of these things behold;
I send My Father's promise, so you must stay.
Until you have received the power from on high,
He blessed them and went away.

And it came to pass, while He blessed them he was
parted from them and carried up into heaven.
(Luke 24:51)

JOHN

The Samaritans Believed

The Samaritan woman left her water pot and ran
Into the city, to tell of this Man.
"Come, see a man who has told me all
That I have done," she said as she ran.

In the mean while, His disciples returned
Saying, "Come Master and eat."
Said He to them, "You do not know
but I already have meat."

My meat is to do the will of Him that
Sent Me, and to finish His work.
Don't wait four months for the harvest.
It is time right now to harvest the earth.

He that reaps receives wages and gathers
Fruit unto life eternal; you make rejoice together
One sow the other reaps I sent you to reap
Of the crowds that shall gather.

Many of the Samaritans of that city believed in Him,
Because of the testimony of the woman.
They sought Him and He lingered there.
They knew this man was not common.

(John 4:28-39)

Many believed because of His own word;
(John 4:41)

The Day of the Feast

Jesus said, "I will be with you, yet for
A little while longer, then I shall go away.
I shall go back home to Him that sent
Me, for He didn't come here to stay.

You shall seek Me and shall not find
Me, and where I am you cannot come.
This greatly troubled the people, saying
"Where does He go, whom does He disperse among?"

In the last day, that great day of the feast,
Jesus stood and cried, "If any thirst, come to Me.
He that believes in Me, as the scripture
Has said, rivers of water will flow from his belly."

This spoke He of the Spirit, those
Who believe on Him could receive.
The Holy Ghost was not yet given, because
Jesus had not been glorified, you just had to believe.

(John 7)

The First Stone

The Scribes and the Pharisees; here
They come again.
This time they brought an accused
Woman that was full of sin.

This woman is taken in adultery,
And they sat her in the midst.
Master, she was caught in the act;
She should be stoned for this.

Jesus answered saying, He that is
Without sin, then cast the first stone.
Jesus wrote on the ground, when
He looked up, they were gone.

"Woman, where are you're accuser?
Have no man condemned you?
Go and sin no more," he said.
That's what you must do.

(John)

... I am the light of the world; he that follows me,
shall not walk in darkness but shall have the light of life

Verily, Verily

If you continue in My word,
Then you are My disciples indeed.

You shall know the truth, and
The truth shall set you free.

Verily, verily, I say unto you:
Whoever commits sin is a servant of sin.
If the Son makes you free, you are free indeed.
Do good works is what the Father intents.

If God were your Father, you would
Love Me for I come of Him that sent Me.
Why can't you understand, what I'm
Saying to you? The devil helps you to see.

Verily, verily, I say to you, before
Abraham was, I am.
They took up stones to stone Him, but
He hid Himself, passed through them, God's holy Lamb.

(John 8:31-59)

I must work the works of Him that sent Me, while it is day;
the night cometh when no man can work
(John 9:4)

Jesus Wept

"Where have you laid him?" Jesus asked.
They answered, "Come and see."
Jesus wept with them that day
For Lazarus was like His family.

Jesus therefore again, groaning in
Himself was led to the grave.
Said to them, "Take the stone away"
For his grave was in a cave.

"If thou believe thou should see
My Father God's great glory.
And believe He has sent me in His name.
Then there will be another end to this story."

"Lazarus, come forth," and the dead
Lazarus came out, bound in grave clothes.

Jesus said, "loose him," and they fell off

Is how the scripture goes.

When the Pharisees were told of

the miracles Jesus had done,
They began to plot His death
for they knew He was the one.

(John 11:35-48)

The Good Shepherd

I am the good shepherd, the good shepherd,
give His life for the sheep
(John 10:11)

Many believed in Jesus and came to the
Feast; when they heard he was coming,
They took branches from palm trees
Shouted Hosanna, as they were running.

Hosanna, blessed is the King, that
Comes in our Lord's great name.
He comes riding on a young ass, as it
Is written, God sent Him and He came.

The hour has come that the Son of man
Should be glorified, it is Him we must serve.
For if we follow Him, where He is there
We will be also, praise Him with every word.

The hour has come, Father, glorify the name.
Then a voice came from heaven, saying
I have glorified it, and will glorify it again.
This voice of thunder spoke that day.

This voice came not because of Me
But for your sake, so you can see.
And if I be lifted up from the earth,
I will draw all men unto Me.

(John 12)

This he said, signifying what death He should die.
(John 12:33)

The Last Supper

Now before the Passover, when Jesus
Knew that His time was come,
The devil having put into Judas Iscariot's
Heart that he betray the Son.

Jesus rose, after supper, laid His
Garments aside, now this is pretty deep.
He took water, and He kneeled down,
And He began to wash the disciples' feet.

But when He came to Peter, Peter said,
"Lord, Thou shall never wash mine."
"If I don't," said Jesus,
"No part of Me will be thine."

Peter said not only my feet Lord
But my hands, and head as well.
Jesus said, "You are not all clean yet
But only time will tell."

One of you will betray Me;
This truth I do know.
Peter, you'll deny Me three
Times before the cock can crow.

(John 13)

Jesus Prays

Jesus lifted His eyes to heaven and
Said, Father, the hour has come.
Glorify Me, that I may glorify you.
My Father glorify, thy Son.

As you have given the Son, power over
All flesh, that He may give eternal life
That they may know you, the only true God,
And Thy Son, Jesus Christ.

I have given them the word in Thy
Name, which you gave to me.
And they have kept Thy word
And believe I came from Thee.

While I was with them, in the world, I kept
them in Thy name, so we can be as one.
Holy father keep them through Thy
Name, so none are lost, because they love the Son.

I pray not for them to be taken out
Of the world, but keep them from evil,
Sanctify them, My Father, through truth,
Truth will shame the devil.

(John 17)

His Time Has Come

Judas, who betrayed Jesus knew
Just where the garden was.
He brought them this band of men
As an enemy oft times does.

Jesus therefore knowing all things
Went forth and said unto them,
"Whom seek thee?" "Jesus of Nazareth"
Was their reply; He said, "I am He."

Jesus answered, "I have told you
I am He, if you are seeking Me.
Let the others go their way, for
I have told you, I am He."

Then Simon Peter, who had a sword
drew it and smote the high Priest's ear.
"Put up your sword," Jesus said.
They bound Him, and led Him away from here.

This is the cup My Father has given
Me, shall I not drink it?
He knew that it was His time.
He complained not even a little bit.

(John 18)

The Cock Crew

Now, Simon Peter followed Jesus, and
So did another disciple; the high Priest knew
Peter stood outside the door, the other
Disciple spoke, and they let Peter through.

Said the damsel at the door, art thou
Not one of the disciples, Peter said "Not I."
He then stood at the fire with the others
Warming themselves, they asked, but Peter lied.

They asked Peter if it were he that had
Cut off the high Priest's ear, he said "No."
It was the third time they had asked
And immediately the cock did crow.

So that the saying that Jesus spoke be
Fulfilled, signifying, how He should die.
They asked if He were the King of the Jews
Jesus said, I speak the truth, for I cannot lie.

Pilate said I find in Him no fault
At all, but shall I release Him unto you?
They all cried, not this man, let the
Robber go, so Pilate did as they said to do.

Peter then denied again: and immediately the cock crew
(John 18:27)

It is Finished

Then the soldiers when they had
Crucified Jesus took His clothes.
They divided them into four parts.
But they threw lots for His coat.

Now standing by the cross was
His mother whom He loved, with a few more women.
Said He, "Woman behold thy son" and
To His disciple, "Behold thy mother" they took her home then.

After this Jesus, knowing all things were
Now accomplished that scripture be fulfilled
Said, "I thirst" they put vinegar to His lips.
He said, "It is finished" and He died on the hill.

They did not break His legs, as they did to
The other two, but they pierced Him in the side.
Out came blood and water, the scripture
is fulfilled for now Jesus had died.

They placed Him in the tomb of Joseph
With a huge stone to block the door.
With guards standing outside to keep away
Anyone from stealing Him, just to be sure.

(John 19)

So when Jesus had received the sour wine, He said "it is finished" and bowing His head He gave up His Spirit
(John 19:30)

THE ACTS

The Almighty Holy Ghost

And when the day of Pentecost was
Fully come, they were on one accord.
Suddenly, there came a mighty wind
From heaven like a mighty wind was poured.

It filled all the house where they were sitting.
It appeared unto them, a cloved tongue like fire.
It filled them with the Holy Ghost and spoke
In other tongues as the spirit did desire.

There were many nations gathered there
For the multitude came together.
They were confounded because each heard
His own language as it came from heaven.

They were all amazed some thought
Them all drunk with wine.
Peter said we're not drunken but,
Filled with the Holy Ghost divine.

And it shall come to pass that whosoever shall
call on the name of the Lord, shall be saved.
(Acts 2:21)

Lies and Death

A certain man named Ananias
With Sapphira his wife
Sold a possession, but kept back
A portion of the price.

He plotted with his wife then lay
A certain part at the apostle's feet.
Peter asked him why has Satan filled
Your head, so you feel you must deceive?

You are trying to lie to the Holy Ghost and
Keep back part of the price for the land.

You conceived in your heart to lie, not only
To man, but to God, at least you think you can.

Ananias when he heard these words fell
Down, gave up the ghost, and he died.
The young men carried him out and buried him,
But they didn't tell his wife.

Not knowing this, his wife also
Said they sold the land for only so much.
She fell down at Peter's feet.
She too lied and yielded the ghost up.

*Then fell she down straightway at his feet, and
the young men came in, and found her dead, and
carrying her forth, buried her by her husband.*
(Acts 5:10)

Acts of the Apostles

Luke wrote in this book about
The Apostles and their acts.
From the time Jesus was taken up,
They saw Him when He went back.

He told them to wait for the promise
Of His Father, to be Holy Ghost baptized,
And how the chosen ones was to
Spread the Word of God, far and wide.

When the day of Pentecost was fully come,
The Holy Spirit gave them utterance.
How men of every nation under heaven
Spoke together and none so much as stuttered.

How your daughters and sons shall prophesy,
And the old men shall dream, dreams.
How God will show wonders and sign.
How we that are saved, will know what it means.

Acts tells of Peter and John, of healings, baptizing,
And even going to jail.
They spoke to the people and their
Rulers and Elders of Israel.

They spoke the Word of God, and
They spoke the Word with boldness
Of Ananias and Sapphira, how they tried
To hide money from the land, when they sold it.

Of Peter and John being put in a common
Prison, and an angel brought them out.
How the chief priest and the captain o

The temple was left with some doubt.

And daily in the temple, and in every house,
that ceased not to teach and preach Jesus Christ.
(Acts 5:42)

Paul and Barnabas Depart

Acts tells us of Paul and Barnabas
How they preached throughout the land.
How Barnabas departed from Paul,
Then Silas became his right-hand man.

It tells of a woman named Lydia who
Loved the Lord, and was a purple seller.
How she and her whole household was baptized,
Worshipped God, because it was better.

And it came to pass, a damsel with
A spirit of divination met Paul and Silas.
She made her masters much gain.
Following Paul, he told her to be silent.

He turned to the spirit and commanded
In the name of Jesus Christ come out of her.
When her masters saw their gain was gone, they
Had them beat, and thrown in jail, yes this did occur.

They were thrown in the inner prison
With their feet fast in the stocks.
They sang and prayed unto God, then an earthquake
Shook and gave the jailers quite a shock.

Although the doors opened up and the
Band on everyone was loosed,
The jailer found they did not leave. cried
I want to be saved, baptized, and used.

He took them and washed their stripes;
Then brought them home and fed them meat.

The magistrate came themselves, to tell them
They could leave and they didn't have to sneak.

Paul waited for Silas and Timotheus in
Athens and his spirit was stirred.
When he saw the city worshipping idols,
He met with them and gave them the Word.

When they heard of the resurrection of the dead,
Some mocked others listened to what he said.
These men clave to him and believed, but to
The unbelievers said he, your blood is on your heads.

*... your blood be upon your own heads; I am clean:
from henceforth I will go unto the Gentiles.*
(Acts 18:6)

ROMANS

The Book of
Romans

Paul wrote Romans, although he was
Not in Rome at the time.
Grace to you and peace from God our
Father and Jesus Christ, Lord of mine.

For God is my witness whom I serve
With my spirit in the gospel of His Son.
I pray and make mention of you in my
Prayers that the will of God to you will come.

I would not have you ignorant, brethren
For I long to import unto you a spiritual gift.
That I might have some fruit among you
That mutual faith gives both of us a lift.

I am not ashamed of the gospel of

Christ for it is salvation unto God's power.
For it is righteousness revealed from faith
To faith which makes unrighteousness cower.

(Rom. 1)

Who changed the truth of God into a lie, and
worshipped and served the creature more than
the Creator, who is blessed forever, Amen
(Rom. 1:25)

Going Against Nature

Who changed the truth of God into a lie,
And served creature more than the Creator?
For this cause, God gave them up unto
Vile affections which is against nature.

Likewise also the men leaving the natural
Use of women, and lust toward another man
Did not like to retain God in their
Knowledge was filled with evil on every hand

God gave them over to reprobate minds
Being filled with all unrighteousness
Full of envy, hate, wickedness, evilness,
Disobedient to parents, unmerciful, and the rest.

Who knowing the judgment of God, that
They commit such things are worthy of death.
Not only the doers of such, but those that
Enjoy the ones that take these steps.

(Rom. 1:25-32)

Who knowing the judgment of God...
... not only do the same, but have
pleasure in them that do them.
(Rom. 1:32)

Judge Not

Therefore thou art inexcusable,
O man that judges another.
You condemns yourself for you that
Judge do the same as the others

You can be sure that the judgment of

God is according to truth against them.
Know this O man, you who do the same
As them, you can't escape from Him.

Or hate the riches of his goodness and
Forbearance, and longsuffering, indeed!
Not knowing God leads you to repent
Will render every man according to His lead.

Tribulation and anguish upon every
Soul of man that do evil.
There is no respect of person with God
He will judge all of His people.

(Rom. 2:1-11)

Justified by Faith

Therefore being justified by faith
Through Jesus Christ with God we have peace.
By whom also we have access by faith into
This grace where we stand in hope, so unique.

We glory in tribulations knowing tribulation
Works patience, and patience works experience, thus
Experience works hope which make not
Ashamed for the Holy Ghost could never hinder us.

Christ died for the ungodly
Scarcely for a righteous man would one die.
For while we were yet sinners
By His blood we were justified.

For we were reconciled to God by the
Death of His Son, we shall be saved by
Wherefore by one mans sin His life entered the world
By death passing to all men redemption by Jesus Christ.

... and so death passed upon all men for that all have sinned
(Rom. 5:12)

God Forbid

What shall we say then, shall we continue
In sin that grace may abound? God forbid!
How shall we that are dead to sin live
Any longer therein? Your sin is not hid.

Know that so many of us as were baptized.
Unto Jesus Christ were baptized unto His death.
By baptism, we are buried with Him that as
Christ we too are risen in newness of life with health.

We have been planted together in the likeness o
His death, we shall also in the likeness of resurrection.
To destroy the body of sin, for he that is dead
Is free from sin, His death made that correction.

Now if we be dead with Christ being
Raised from the dead, dies no more.

Death has no dominion over Him.
He lives, of that you can be sure.

Likewise reckon ye also yourselves to be dead indeed, unto
sin, but alive into God through Jesus Christ our Lord
(Rom. 6:11)

The Wages of Sin is Death

The wages of sin is death, a death with
No hope of resurrection, know this
The gift of God through Jesus Christ is eternal life
Everlasting life through holiness.

For when we were in the flesh, the
Motions of sin worked to bring death forth
For the law says thou shall not covet
The flesh brings forth lust.

There is therefore now no condemnation to
Them which is in Christ, that walks not after the flesh
But walks after the Spirit, for the law
Of the spirit, of life in Christ, makes us stand the test.

The law was weak through the flesh, until
God sent His own Son
He came in the likeness of sinful flesh
To condemn sin, and to save everyone.

(Rom. 6-8)

That the righteousness of the law might be fulfilled in us,
who walk not after the flesh, but after the spirit.
(Rom. 8:4)

A Thankful Day

Be thankful as this day is celebrated.
Keep God on your mind and lips.
Be thankful for the life He has given us.
Young and old, know life is a gift.

Let us walk honestly in the day.
Not in strife and envying.

Be thankful for God's bounty.
Praise Jesus for He's the King.

He that regards the day regards it unto.
The Lord, He that gives God thanks.
For this end Christ died and rose to be
Lord to the dead and the living Saint.

Every knee shall bow and every tongue
Confess so each shall be accountable.
The kingdom of God is not meat and drink
But righteousness, and peace, abounds for us.

(Rom. :13-14)

... but righteousness and peace, and joy, in the Holy Ghost
(Rom. 14:17)

1 CORINTHIANS

To the Church

Paul's Letter to the
Church of Corinth
I thank God always in your behalf

Paul wrote to the church of Corinth
That in everything you are enriched by Him
Through Jesus Christ, the Son, He sent.

I beseech you brethren in Jesus's name
That you all speak the same thing.
And that there be no division among you
But join together in minds of the same.

Because the foolishness of God is wiser
Than men, and His weakness is much stronger.
For you see, your callings brethren
God will have you foolish no longer.

He has chosen the weak things of the world
To confound the things that are mighty.
That no flesh should glory in His presence
And he that glorify do not do it lightly.

But of Him are ye in Jesus Christ, who of God,
is made unto us wisdom and righteousness
and sanctification, and redemption:
(1 Cor. 1:30)

Labor Together

Brethren, I speak to you as unto carnal
I have fed you with milk
For meat you cannot handle yet
Being yet carnal, there is a rift.

For among you, there is still envy
And strife, you walk as men.
You are divided one from another
Some believe yet some still sin.

While one says, I am of Paul
For I have planted the seed.
Some who are of Apollos, who waters, we
Are nothing, for God gives the increase.

He that planted and he that watered
Are one, and each receives his own reward
According to his own labor
Laboring together with God ain't hard.

(1 Cor. 3:1-9)

For we are laborers together with God...
(1 Cor. 3:9)

And ye are Christ's and Christ is God's
(1 Cor. 3:23)

Sexual Sin

It is reported commonly that there is
Fornication among you, the Gentiles not so much.
That one should have his father's wife
And you are all puffed up.

For I verily, as absent in body, but present in
Spirit have judged already, as if I were there
In the name of our Lord, Jesus Christ
When you gather, His power is everywhere

Keep not company with fornicators or
Idolaters, or drunkards, nor judge them that are within
Therefore put away from among yourselves
That wicked person filled with sin.

Know ye not that the bodies are members of

Christ, shall I also share it with the harlot?
God forbid! He that is joined unto the Lord is
One spirit, flee fornicators, we know ye not.

For ye are bought with a price; therefore glorify God
in body and in your spirit, which are God's.
(1 Cor. 6:20)

Better to Marry

How important is it to marry?
The unmarried and widows must learn.
It is good for them to marry
For it is better to marry than to burn.

To the unmarried woman who departs
From her husband, you must remain alone.
For if you desire to have a companion,
Then you must return back home.

Also husbands, do not put away your
Wife, who do not believe.
Likewise the unbelieving husband
Is not a reason to leave.

For the unbelieving husband or
The unbelieving wife, is sanctified by each,
Whereas your children who were unclean are
Now holy, for God has called you to peace.

(1 Cor. 7)

*For what knowest thou, O wife,
whether thou shall save the husband?
Or how knowest thou O man, whether
thou shall save thy wife?*
(1 Cor. 7:16)

Run the Race

Know ye this my brothers and sisters
They that run in a race, run all
Only one can receive the prize
You must run on as others stall.

Some start out fast, and set a pace
But soon they began to wan.
While others run steadily
Because this is the way they've trained.

The race in not given to the swift
But to the ones who endures to the end.
As others drop out around you
Those who take a shortcut to sin.

God's people are steadily running,
Keeping their eyes on the prize.
Forward ever forward, keeping
The finish line in their sights.

... but we are incorruptible
(1 Cor. 9:25)

Be Worthy

For I have received of the Lord
That which I delivered unto you
That the same night in which
He was betrayed, this He did do.

When He gave thanks, he brake bread
Saying; Take eat, this is my body.
Do this in remembrance of Me.
After the same manner, He took the cup
Saying: This cup is the New Testament in
My blood, do ye often in remembrance of Me.

For as often as ye drink this cup and eat,
This bread shows the Lord's death until He comes.
Examine yourselves and be worthy
Eat and drink not, if this can't be done.

For he that eats and drinks unworthy
Bring damnation to himself.
Causing many to be sick and to die.
So take time to examine ourselves.

(1 Cor. 11)

For as often as ye eat this bread, and drink this
cup, ye do shew the Lord's death till He comes.
(1 Cor. 11:26)

Charity

Although I speak with tongues
Of men and angels, but have no charity,
I become as sounding brass or a
Tinkling cymbal, for you can't understand me.

Though I have the gift of prophecy
And understand all mysteries
With all knowledge and faith that I have,
I'm nothing without charity.

Charity suffers long and is kind.
Charity envies not and is not puffed up.
Does not act unseemly, brags not or is.
Not easily provoked, thinks no evil or other muck.

Charity rejoices in truth and never fails.
While prophecies, knowledge, and tongues fade away.
When I was a child, I spoke as a child.
But as a man, childish things I do not say.

Now abides faith, hope, charity, and of

These three
Of them all, the greatest of them
Is charity.

(1 Cor. 14)

Let all things be done decently and in order
(1 Cor. 14:40)

We Shall Live Again

If Christ preached that He rose from the dead,
How can you say there's no resurrection?
Did Christ not arise? Then
I offer you all this correction.

If Christ be not risen, then our preaching
Is in vain and your faith too is in vain.
And those that have testified of God, that
He raised up Christ, is just some type of game.

Then those who died in Christ are perished.
If in this life only we have hope in Christ,
Then we are all men most miserable.
And we are living a miserable life.

But Christ did rise from His grave and
Is alive and as in Adam we all die.
Even so in Christ Jesus we shall all
Be made alive, and be with Him in the sky.

(1 Cor. 15)

For he must reign, till he hath put all enemies under his feet
(1 Cor. 15:25)

The last enemy that shall be destroyed is death
(1 Cor. 15:26)

2 CORINTHIANS

2 Corinthians
By Faith not Sight

Know that He who raised up the Lord
Jesus shall also raise us up too.
For all things are for our sakes, with
Abundant grace, gives God cause to raise you.

For which cause we faint not, but our outward
Man perish and inward man is renewed.
Day by day, inward man, renewed, work more exceeding
By the weight of glory, isn't that good news?

We look not at things which are seen
But at things that are not seen.
For the things which are seen are temporal,
While those which are not seen are eternal things.

For we walk by faith not by sight.
Therefore we are always confident knowing that
While we are home in the body, we are absent
From the Lord, so earth takes this body back.

Therefore any man be in Christ, he is a new creature,
old things are passed away; behold all things become new.
(2 Cor. 5:17)

Giving to God

He who sows sparingly shall reap sparingly.
He who sows bountifully shall reap more.
Every man according as he purpose in his heart
To give not grudgingly, God opens the door

For God loves a cheerful giver, and He is
Able to make all grace, abound toward you.
That you having all sufficiency in all things
May abound to every good work too.

Now he that ministers seed to the sower
Also ministers bread for your food.
Multiplies your sown seed and increase the fruit,
Enrich bounties causes thanksgiving to God through you.

And by their prayer for you which
Long after God's exceeding grace.
Thanks be unto God, for His unspeakable
Gift, His gospel keeps us in this race.

... they glorify God for your professed
subjection unto the gospel of Christ...
(2 Cor. 9:13)

GALATIANS

Galatians

Paul, an apostle, not of man, but by
Jesus Christ and God the Father,
Who raised Jesus from the grave.
Grace be with you, and peace to you, my brother.

Our Lord Jesus Christ gave Himself for
Our sins that He may deliver us from evil.
According to the Father's will,
Jesus died to save the weak and feeble.

As we said before, so say I now again.
If any man preach any other gospel to you,
Let him be accursed, for I seek not to
Please men, but God, in all that I say and do.

The gospel that I preach is not after man for
I neither received it of man or by man was taught it.
But by the revelation of Jesus Christ,
I was called by His grace, by Him, the fire was lit.

I lived with Peter fifteen days, and except
For James, the Lord's brother,
I saw no apostles except for them
I didn't see the others.

(Gal. 1)

... behold before God, I lie not
(Gal. 1:20)

(and they glorified God in me
(Gal. 1:24)

Live in the Spirit

This I say, walk in the spirit and ye shall
Not fulfill the lust of the flesh.
Being contrary against each other,
The flesh will manifest:

Adultery, fornication, uncleanness, idolatry,
Witchcraft, hatred, and strife,
Sedition, heresies, envying, murders,
Drunkenness, just a sinful life.

But the fruit of the spirit is love,
Joy, peace, longsuffering, and faith,
Gentleness, goodness, meekness, temperance,
Against these, no laws can break.

And they that are Christ's have crucified
The flesh, with the affections and lusts.
Let us walk in the spirit, and the
Ways of the world cannot touch us.

(Gal. 5)

If we live in the spirit, let us walk in the spirit.
(Gal. 5:26)

EPHESIANS

The Epistle of Paul to the Ephesians

Blessed be the God and Father of our Lord,
Jesus who has blessed us in heavenly places.
He has chosen us in Him before the world
Foundation, in love, that we are blameless races.

Having predestinated us the adoption of

Children by Jesus Christ Himself.
According to the good pleasures of His will
Redemption through His blood, we need nothing else.

Redemption through His blood, we have forgiveness of

Sins, according to the riches of His grace
We bring heirs obtained an inheritance
According to His purpose, for heaven's sake.

Praise His glory, in whom you also trusted
After you heard, the word of truth.
After that you were sealed with the Holy
Spirit of promise, which Jesus gave to you.

In whom ye also trusted after that ye heard the
word of truth, the gospel of your salvation...
(Eph. 1:13)

Good Works

For by grace are we saved.
Through faith it is God's gift.
Not of works lest any man should
Boast, with proud lips.

We are God's workmanship created
In Jesus Christ, unto good works.
God has ordained that we should work
His good works we shall birth

Without Christ, the covenants of promise
Have no hope, and without God in the world
But now by the blood of Jesus Christ, our Peace
We are able as one to give Him a whirl.

We build upon the foundation of the prophets, and
Apostles, Jesus being the chief corner stone
Built together for God's habitation through
The Spirit, we are God's own.

... it is the gift of God: not of works,
lest any man should boast
(Eph. 2:8,9)

Walk in the Light

Be renewed in the spirit of your
Mind, put on the new man,
Which God created in righteousness.
And true holiness, only the new man can.

Put away lying, speak with
Your neighbor only the truth.
For we are members one to another
Teach this to all the group.

Be angry, and sin not, do not.
Let the sun go down on your wrath.
Neither give peace to the devil
No more stealing, corruption, or graft.

Put away, wrath, anger, and evil speaking
With all malice, as well.
Be kind one to another, tenderhearted, and
Forgiving as we take a detour from hell.

Be ye therefore followers of God as dear children;
And walk in love...
(Eph. 5:1, 2)

Christ is the Head

Christ is the head of the church and
Is the Savior of the body, give thanks.
Submitting yourselves one to another
Soberly, for being drunk with wine, stank.

Wives submit yourselves unto your own
Husband for the husband is the wives head.
Therefore as the church is subject to Christ
Your husband is by whom you are led.

Husbands love your wives, even as Christ
Also loves the church, and gave Himself for it.
That He may cleanse it by washing, by the Word,
To present to Himself a church without blemish.

So love your wives, as yourselves
For no man hates his own flesh.
But nourish, and cherish, your wives
Be as one, Jesus said this is best.

Children obey your parents in
The Lord, for this is right.
Honor them, which is the first commandment
With promise, for a longer life.

(Eph. 5-6:1)

This is a great mystery but I speak
concerning Christ and the church
(Eph. 5:32)

PHILIPPIANS

The Epistle of Paul to the Philippians

Paul, while waiting for trial in prison,
sent the Philippians a thank-you letter
Grace be with you and peace, for
your gift has made me feel better.

I thank God upon every thought of you,
for your fellowship in the gospel everyday.
I am confident of a good work, begun in you,
performed Jesus Christ's way.

I pray that your love may abound, more
and more in knowledge and in all judgment,
without offence until the day of Christ,
filled with the fruit of righteousness, by His strength.

As always, Christ shall be magnified in
my body, whether by life or by death.
For to live is Christ, and to die is gain.
I can choose nothing else.

*For I am in a strait betwixt two, having a desire to
depart, and be with Christ; which is far better*
(Phi 1:23)

... nevertheless to abide in the flesh, is more needful for you
(Phi 1:2)

Run Not in Vain

At the name of Jesus every knee should bow,
of things in heaven, earth, and below
Every tongue should confess, that Jesus Christ
is Lord, to the glory of God, don't you know?

It is God that works in you, both to
will and to do of His good pleasure.
Do all things without murmuring and disputing,
rejoicing in your faith, I, joy in heaven's treasure.

Holding forth the word of life, that I may rejoice
in the day of Christ, that I have not run in vain.

But I trust in the Lord, to send you Timotheus,
to show you God's good things

Beware of dogs, beware of evil workers,
for we who worship God in spirit do rejoice.
Have no confidence in the flesh, but walk
in the spirit, it is the only choice.

(Phi 3:2-3)

For we are the circumcision, which worship
God in the spirit, and rejoice in Christ Jesus,
and have no confidence in the flesh
(Phi 3:3)

God Supplies Our Needs

Finally brethren, whatsoever things
are honest, whatsoever things are true,
whatsoever things are pure and just
and of good report, think on the things you do.

Those things which you have, both learned
and received that you heard from me.
And the things you've seen me do, know the
God of peace shall be with you, and always will be.

I have learned in whatever state
I am, I am to be content.
I know how to be full and to be hungry for I
can do all things through Christ, He gives me strength.

My God shall supply all your needs,
according to His riches in Glory.
God's grace be with you all forever.
This is a never-ending story,
Amen.

(Phi 4)

COLOSSIANS

The Epistle of Paul to the Colossians

Ephesians, Philippians, Colossians, and Philemon
are sometimes called the "Prison Epistles"
because Paul wrote to them while still awaiting trial.
The news he had heard of Colosse
made him stop and think awhile.

He had never been to their church,
but after hearing their troubling news,
he wrote them this letter; although still
in prison he was still being used.

He wrote to saints and faithful brethren
Grace be with you and peace
our dear fellow servant, who love Christ.
It's you I'm trying to reach.

We do not cease to pray for you, and ask
that with knowledge you be filled.
Walk worthy of the Lord, pleasing Him,
for this is the Lord's will.

(Col 1)

That ye might walk worthy of the Lord, unto
all pleasing, being fruitful in every good work,
and increasing in knowledge of God
(Col 1:10)

1 THESSALONIANS

The First Epistle of Paul to the Thessalonians

Grace be with you and peace from God
the Father and Jesus Christ, we give thanks.
We always mention you in our prayers,
for to forget your works of faith, I just can't.

For our gospel came not unto you in
word only, but in Holy Ghost power,
that you have spread your faith
in each place, from that very hour.

For you, brethren, know our meeting
with you was not in vain.
For our teachings were not deceit or uncleanness,
or guile, but of God, was made plain.

You are witnesses as was God, how holily
and justly, and we were well behaved.
For you became followers of the churches
of God, and to righteousness, to Him we've become slaves.

(1Th 1)

For what is our hope or joy or crown of rejoicing?...
(1Th 1:19)

For ye are our glory and joy
(1Th 1:20)

Good Advice

Furthermore, we urge you brethren, and advice
strongly, that you walk to please God more and more.
You know the commandments, given by the
Lord, Jesus, and just what sin has in store.

The will of God and your sanctification
should abstain you from sexual sin.
Everyone of you should possess his own vessel
in sanctification and honor, not lust, like sinner men.

For God has not called us unto uncleanness,
but unto holiness, so when you hate, you hate Him.
But as loving, brothers, you love one another
being taught of God, to love all of them.

If we believe Jesus died and rose again,
even the dead in Him will rise.
When the Lord, Himself, descends from heaven,
the dead and those alive will meet Him in the skies.

(1Th 4)

Then we which are alive and remain shall be caught
up together with them in the clouds, to meet the Lord
in the air; and so shall we ever be with the Lord
(1Th 4:17)

Watch and Be Sober

There is no need for me to tell you
of the times and of the seasons.
You, yourself, know the Lord comes as a thief,
in the night, no set time just His reason.

You, brethren, are not in darkness, that
that day should surprise you.
You are children of the day not night,
therefore sleep not, as others do.

Let us watch and be sober, for
the drunkard sleeps in the night.
Putting on the breastplate of faith and
love, and with a helmet, we are ready for the fight.

God has appointed us salvation, He who died
for us so we could live with Him.
Warn the unruly, comfort the feeble minded,
support the weak, be patient with all of them.

See that none render evil for evil unto any man;
but ever follow that which is good...
(1Th 5:15)

Grace Be with You

Rejoice evermore, pray without ceasing.
In every thing give thanks, this is God's will.
Quench not the spirit, despise not prophesying,
even if it's a bitter pill.

Prove all things, with the word, hold
fast to that which is good.
Do not appear to be evil, and the very God
of peace will sanctify you, as He said He would.

I pray that you be blameless, unto the
coming, your whole body and soul.
Faithful is He that calls you, greet all with
a holy kiss, I charge you that you've been told.

Read this epistle to every holy
brother, grace be with you then.
The Lord God's continued blessings
Christ be with you all, Amen.

(1Th 5)

Greet all brethren with a holy kiss
(1Th 5:26)

2 THESSALONIANS

The Second Epistle of Paul to the Thessalonians
THE SECOND LETTER

Shortly after Paul wrote the first Thessalonians,
Paul heard there was still concern.
So he wrote the second letter to them,
to explain and help them to learn.

Grace unto you and peace from
God, our Father, and the Lord, Jesus Christ.
We thank God, always for you, and
now we must set things right.

To you who are troubled when the Lord
and His angels from heaven be revealed
When He shall come to be glorified to
His saints and His calling be fulfilled.

That the name of our Lord, Jesus Christ
may be glorified in you, and you in Him.
According to His grace, and love know this,
He will not leave you out on a limb.

... that our God would count you worthy of His calling...
(2Th 1:11)

Concerning the Coming

Now concerning the coming of Jesus Christ
and our gathering together unto Him, here.
Let your minds not be troubled, neither by
Spirit nor word that the day of the Lord is near.

Let no man deceive you by any means,
for that day shall not come.
Except the falling away comes first, and
the man of sin, be revealed as perdition son.

Who opposes and exalts himself above all
that is called God or that is worshipped.

He sits in the temple of God, showing himself

to be God, don't let your soul be purchased.

He shall be taken out of the way and that
wicked be revealed, and by God, consumed.
The spirit of His mouth shall destroy
by God's brightness, darkness is so doomed.

That they all might be damned who believed not the truth...
(2Th 2:12)

1 TIMOTHY

The First Epistle of Paul to Timothy

Timothy had been in Paul's evangelistic
team for quite a number of years.
Timothy had to go to Macedonia to
teach the qualities of the overseers.

Paul wanted Timothy to teach them to
use the laws for the disobedient and lawless.
The ungodly sinners, who defile themselves
with whoremongers, liars, and ungodliness.

Anything that is contrary to sound doctrine
according to the glorious gospel,
God has counted me faithful, and
not to sin, I am ever to be watchful.

Jesus Christ came into the world to
save sinners, of whom I am chief.
But I have obtained mercy
in Him, hereafter I have belief.

Now unto the king, eternal, immortal, invisible, the only
wise God, be honour and glory for ever and ever, amen
(1Ti 1:17)

Pray for All Men

I exhort first of all that intercession
prayer be made for all men.
That the kings, and those in authority may
be godly and honest, and stay away from sin/

For this is good and acceptable
in our Savior, God's sight,
who would have all men to be saved
unto the knowledge of truth, and living right.

For there is one God, and one mediator
between God and those in sin.
The man Jesus Christ, who gave Himself,
a ransom, to save our lives, back then.

I will therefore that men pray everywhere,
lifting up your holy hands.
Without wrath and doubting in
like manner also a modest and sober woman.

... lifting up holy hands without wrath and doubting
(1Ti 2:8)

2 TIMOTHY

Timothy's Second Letter
Paul wrote his second letter to Timothy

while in jail again, and he was all alone.
Being a Christian was a crime, so
they weren't quick to be known.

Paul thanked God for His grace, mercy,
and peace, also Jesus as he always did.
He served with a pure conscience without
ceasing, openly, his prayers were not hid.

He called to his remembrance how God was with
his mother Eunice and Lois his grandmother.
May their genuine faith, in God the Father
dwell within you, my brother.

He remembered that to Timothy, to
stir up the gift of God, by putting on hands.
For He has not given us the spirit of fear
but our sound minds will stand.

Be not ashamed of the testimony of

our Lord nor of me, His prisoner.
He has saved us and called us with a holy calling,
not by our works, to tell every listener.

(2Ti 1)

Depart from Inquity

It is a faithful saying: For if we be dead
with him, we shall also live with Him.
If we suffer, we also reign with Him.
If we deny Him, He will deny us, Tim.

If we believe not, yet He stays faithful.
He cannot deny Himself, remember this.
Study to prove yourself approved unto God,
shunning profane, vain babbling, and ungodliness.

Some concerning the truth have already
erred, their words eaten as a canker worm.
Saying the resurrection is past already
they overthrow the faith of some.

But the foundation of God stands
sure, having this seal.
The Lord knows those that belong to
Him and He knows us, that are real.

... and let everyone that nameth the name
of Christ depart from iniquity
(2Ti 2:19)

Know This

Know this also, in the last days
perilous times will come.
Men shall love themselves, be covetous,
boastful, and disobedient to dad and mom.

Unthankful and unholy, false accusers
and despisers, without natural affection.
They will love pleasures more than God.
They will turn away from His protection.

They'll be ever learning and never
able to come to the knowledge of truth.
Men of corrupt minds, reprobate concerning
the faith, real, real easy to dupe.

But those who fully know my doctrine
manner of life, charity, and longsuffering,
know I endured, and through them all
the Lord God, has delivered me.

Yea, all that live Godly, in Christ Jesus,
shall suffer persecution
(2Ti 3:12)

But evil men and seducers, shall wax worse and worse,
deceiving and being deceived
(2Ti 3:13)

TITUS

The Epistle of Paul to Titus

Paul gave to Titus guidelines for preaching,
according to the faith of God's elect,
acknowledging the truth
that is after godliness.

In hope of eternal life which God, who cannot lie,
promised before the world began,
has manifested His word though preaching
according to our Savior's commands.

He gave to Titus also, the qualifications for
a bishop to be a good and just man.
Sober, blameless, keeping the word of God,
and helping others to understand.

Unto the pure all things are pure: but to the
defiled and unbelieving nothing is.
Because their minds and conscience is defiled
they disobey, which is not God's will.

Tit 1

Unto the pure all things are pure: but unto them that
are defiled and unbelieving is nothing pure;...
(Tit 1:15)

Elders

Older men be sober, grave, saved in faith,
patience, and in charity too.
The aged woman likewise in your
behavior be holy, as God tells you to do.

Teach the younger woman to also be
sober, to treat their husbands and children right.
Being obedient to their own husbands
through God, being a guiding light.

Young men likewise be sober minded
showing a pattern of good works.

That no evil thing is said against you,
for salvation your heart must search.

Deny ungodliness, and worldly lust,
we must live soberly, righteous, and just,
living for the glorious Savior
Jesus Christ gave His life for us.

Tit 2

PHILEMON

The Epistle of Paul to Philemon

A slave, Onesimus, had run away from
his master, Philemon, and met Paul.
He was converted, then Paul persuaded
him to return to Philemon, and stand tall.

Paul wrote:, Hearing of your love and
the faith you have for all saints
and your acknowledgement of all good
things, through Christ, continued running, he can't.

For we have great joy and consolation in
thy love because the saints are refreshed by you.
Yet for love's sake I come to you on behalf of

Onesimus, please receive him, he'll pay his dues.

If you count me as a partner, receive him
as myself, although he parted for a season.
Receive him not as a servant, but a brother
in the Lord, receive him for this reason.

If he has wronged you, or owe you
put it on my account, Paul wrote.
The grace of our Lord Jesus Christ, be with
your spirit, he gave Onesimus this note.

Phm

HEBREWS

Hebrews

God in times past, spoke to the fathers
by the prophets in various manners.
But in these last days, He spoke to us,
through His Son, and Heir, of all that mattered.

His Son, being the brightness of His glory and
image, holding all things by the word of His power.
When He had purged our sins, sat down
at the right hand of the Majesty, from whom angels cower.

Being made so much better than the angels, by
inheritance obtained a more excellent name than they
"This day I will be His Father, and He
will be to me a Son" is what God had to say.

Let all the angels of God worship Him,
unto the Son, this is what He said.
Thy throne, O God, is forever and ever
by Jesus Christ we are led.

The works of the Lord laid the foundation of

the earth and heaven with Thine hands.
They shall perish, but He remains,
and His word shall always stand.

1 chapter

Crowned with Glory

We ought to give earnest heed to
the things which we have heard.
Unless at any time we should let
them slip, then we shall know our word.

For if the word spoken by angels
was steadfast and every transgression just,
how can we escape if we neglect so
great salvation, spoken by the Lord for us?

God also bear them witness both with
signs and wonders with diverse miracles,
and gifts of the Holy Ghost according to His will
that show us the God we serve is not fickle.

But we see Jesus was made a little
lower than the angels for the suffering of death.
Crowned with glory and honor, should taste
death for every man, He gave that of Himself.

*... crowned with glory and honor that He by the
grace of God should taste death for every man*
(Heb 2:9)

The Same Mouth

Out of the same mouth comes
blessing and cursing, how can this be?
Does a fountain send both sweet and bitter water?
Or do olive berries grow on a fig tree?

Does a fountain yield both salt
water and also fresh?
Let a good man with wisdom and knowledge
have conversation and meekness.

But if you are bitter, envying, and
have strife in your heart,
this wisdom is not of heaven, but
the work of the devil, doing his part.

The wisdom that is from above is
first pure, then peaceful, and gentle good fruit.
The fruit of righteousness is sown in
peace for it comes from good roots.

(Heb 3)

And the fruit of righteousness is sown in
peace of them that make peace...
(Heb 3:18)

Fervent Prayers Avails Much

Above all things, my brother, swear not
neither by heaven nor by earth.
Or by any other oath, but let your
yea and nay show your worth.

Is any among you afflicted? Let him pray.
Is any merry? Let him sing psalms.
Is any sick? Then call the elders, let
them pray the anointing over each one.

Anointing them with oil in the name
of the Lord, for the prayers of faith,
they shall save the sick, and He'll lift them up,
forgive their sin, if they'll patiently wait.

Confess your faults one to another,
and pray for each other that you be healed.
The effectual, fervent prayer availed much,
for a devoted earnest prayer is God's will.

And the prayer of faith shall save the sick,
and the Lord shall raise him up;...
(Heb 5:15)

If God Permits

When you ought to be teachers, you
have need that one teach you again,
which is the first principle of God's oracles,
and becomes such need of men.

For such have need of milk and
not of strong meat, not yet.
For everyone that uses milk is unskillful
in the word, as a baby, still on the breast.

But strong meat belongs to them
that are full of age, in other words, grown.

To discern both good and evil,
with the good sense to leave sin alone.

Therefore let us leave the principles of

the doctrine of Christ and go on to perfection,
not laying again the foundation of

repentance from dead works or God's protection.

And of doctrine of baptisms, of laying on
of hands, of resurrection of the dead.
This we will do if He permits,
that is what the word said.

(Heb 5)

This we will do if God permits
(Heb 6:3)

Have Faith

Faith is the substance of things hoped for,
the evidence of things not seen.
Through faith we understand that
worlds were formed by God, us to redeem.

By faith, Abel offered a more excellent sacrifice
than his brother Cain that day,
by which he obtained witness that he
was righteous by God, being dead spoke any way.

By faith, Enoch was translated that he
should not see death and was not found.
No matter how much they looked for him,
he was not around.

By faith, Noah, being warned by God o
things not seen, built the ark.
He saved his household, and the animals.
Faith told him this was no lark.

Without faith it's impossible to please God,
for he that comes to Him must believe.

He rewards those that diligently seek Him.
Faith is all you'll ever need.

By faith, Abraham, when he was called,
he obeyed and he went out.
By faith, an old Sarah conceived,
and birthed Isaac healthy and stout.

By faith, Abraham was tested, offered
up Isaac, for God came before his son.
Knowing God could raise him up. By faith,
Isaac blessed his sons concerning things to come.

By faith, Jacob, when he lay dying,
blessed both of Joseph's sons.
By faith, Joseph, when he died, left
instruction concerning his bones to everyone.

By faith, Moses was hidden three months
by his parents to save his life.
By faith, he became of age and knew that
he must return, for that life just wasn't right.

By faith, he forsook Egypt and kept the
Passover by the sprinkling of the blood,
that death should not touch
God's children whom He loved.

(Heb 11)

But without faith, it is impossible to please Him:...

The Same God Forever

Let brotherly love continue, be not forgetful
to entertain strangers, for you just don't know.
Some have entertained angels unknowing,
so always let your true love show.

Remember to treat those who suffer adversity,
even those that are in chains.
And those who are mistreated as,
if you were indeed the same.

Marriage is honorable among all and
the bed undefiled, fornicators will be judged.
Let your conduct be without covetousness,
because His word you cannot bulge.

God said He would not leave us nor
forsake us, so we may boldly say,
I will not fear what man can do to me
for He's the same God even today.

Jesus Christ the same yesterday, today, and forever
(Heb 13:8)

JAMES

James

Saints, count it all joy when you
fall into diverse temptations.
Knowing this that the trying of

your faith produces patience.

If any of you lack wisdom, let him
ask of God who give to all liberally.
No strings attached, for God's gifts
are given us most diligently.

But we must ask in faith with nothing
wavering as a sea driven by wind.
For if you waver you will receive nothing
from the Lord, nor will double-minded men.

A double-minded man is unstable
in all of his ways.
Blessed is the man who endureth temptation,
the crown of life is his that day.

Wherefore let every man be swift to hear,
slow to speak, and slow to anger or wrath.
Wrath is not the righteousness of God, and
your soul will be lost, now you do the math.

(Jam 1)

A Deadly Tongue

We all stumble in many things if

any man does not stumble in word.
He is a perfect man, able to bridle
the whole body and be deterred.

Behold we put bits in the horses'
mouth that they might obey.
We can by the using of them
turn his body, whichever way.

Also the ships, although they are great
and are driven by fierce winds,
they are turned about, by a small helm
which is controlled by men.

Even the tongue is a little member
but boasts of great things.
It defiles the whole body and set it
on a course to hell, it can be real mean.

The beast, the birds, and the serpents
have all been tamed by mankind.
But the tongue no man can tame, it is
full of poison, that doesn't kill you as you dine.

(Jam 3)

But the tongue can no man tame;
it is an unruly evil full of deadly poison

Resist the World

From where does wars and fighting among
you come from? Are they not from your lusts?
Even your lust that fight in your members
surely, you know not to trust.

You lust and have not, you kill and
desire to have, and cannot obtain.
You fight and war, yet you have nothing
you must ask God if you hope to gain.

But you ask and receive not because
you ask amiss, to consume in your lust.
Do you think the scriptures lie?
The world is God's enemy, therefore a enemy to us.

God resists the proud, but gives grace to
the humble; submit yourselves to him.
Resist the devil, and he will flee from you.
Purify your heart, you double minded, or life is dim.

(Jam 4)

Speak not evil one to another, brethren...
(Jam 4:11)

Being Patient

Be patient until the coming of the Lord.
Look how the farmer waits.
He waits for the precious fruit of

earth, no matter how long it takes.

He is patient until he receives the
early and the latter rain.
Be ye also patient establish your
hearts for His coming reign.

The coming of the Lord draws near,
so grudge not against another.
Less you be condemned, for behold the
Judge stands at the door, my brother.

The prophets have spoken in the name
of the Lord, of suffering, patience, and afflictions.
Behold, we count them happy who have endured and
remained patient through their convictions.

... ye have heard of patience of Job...
(Jam 5:11)

1 PETER

The First Epistle of Peter

We Have Hope Too
Blessed be the God, Father of Jesus Christ
our Lord, grace be with you,
and peace be multiplied, for according
to His abundant mercy, we have hope too.

By Jesus rising from the dead, to an
inheritance, incorruptible and undefiled.
That fade not away, reserved in heaven
for you, Jesus went that extra mile.

For we greatly rejoice, though now
for a season, if need be grieved by trials.
That the true faith being more precious than gold,
that perishes, through praise the Lord allows.

Though it be tried with fire, might
be found unto praise, honor, and glory.
At the appearing of our Lord, Jesus Christ, who
is the beginning and the end of this story.

Whom having not seen, ye love;...
rejoice with joy unspeakable and full of glory
(1Pe 1:8)

Flesh is Like Grass

For all flesh is like grass and all
the glory of man is as a flower.
The grass and flower withers and dies,
but the word of God has staying power.

The word of the Lord endureth forever.
This word is preached by you.
Laying aside all malice and evil, crave the
word, as babies crave milk, live as Jesus did.

If so you have tasted that the Lord
is gracious, chosen of God, and is precious,
you also are lively stones built on a
spiritual house, one that Jesus embraces.

Acceptable to God by Jesus who is the chief

Cornerstone, on Him we believe.
You are a chosen generation, a holy nation,
a peculiar people, who's praises He receives.

Dearly beloved, abstain from fleshly lusts
that war against the soul.
Let your good works shine through,
so that evil doer may behold.

(1Pe :1-2)

Do Good Not Evil

The eyes of the Lord are over the righteous,
and His ears are open to their prayers.
The face of the Lord is against them that
do evil, so do good and you will be spared.

If you are followers of that which is
Good, who will be able to do you harm?
For if you suffer for righteousness sake,
you are safe in our Savior's arms.

Even if they speak evil of you, they
may be ashamed that falsely accuse.
For it is better you suffer for well doing
than evil, it is up to you to choose.

For Christ has also suffered for sin,
for the just and for the unjust.
Being put to death in the flesh to
bring us to the Father, yes all of us.

... by the resurrection of Jesus Christ
(1Pe 3:21)

Who is gone into heaven, and is on the right hand of God...
(1Pe 3:22)

2 PETER

The Lack of Knowledge

He that lacks the knowledge and the
love of our Lord Jesus, is blind then.
For he cannot see afar off and has
forgotten he was purged from his old sins.

Therefore I will always remind you
of these things, although, them you know.
Even after my death you will have these
memories always to take where you go.

For we have not followed cunningly devised tales,
but the power and coming of the Lord.
We were eye witnesses of His majesty and
what He received from His father God.

When a voice came from heaven, saying,
"This is My beloved Son, whom I am well pleased."
What we heard when we were with Him on the
Holy Mount, still brings us to our knees.

*For the prophecy came not in old time by the will of man, but
holy men of God spake as they were moved by the Holy Ghost*
(2Pe 1:21)

The Lord Knows

But there were false prophets also among
the people, and there will be some among you.
Even denying the Lord that brought them
swift destruction is come due.

Many shall follow their pernicious ways
and speak evil of the truth.
God spared not the angels that sinned
and cast them to hell, for their judgment was due.

He spared not the old world, but saved
Noah, a preacher of righteousness.
He brought a flood and wiped out the ungodly,
saving Noah, and his family was blessed.

He turned Sodom and Gomorrha into ashes,
making them an example of them that sin.
But saved Lot, for God knows how to
deliver the godly from the sinful men.

The Lord know how to deliver the godly
out of temptation and punish the unjust.
He's able to deliver the goodly people as
He punishes the ungodly and the corrupt.

(2Pe 2)

1 JOHN

The First Epistle of John
The Truth is the Light

That which was from the beginning which
we have heard and seen with our eyes,
which we have looked upon, touched.
Our hands have handled the word of life

For life was manifested and we have
seen it that was the Son, Jesus Christ.
This is the message we declare to you
in Him there is no darkness, for He is light.

If we say we have no fellowship with Him,
we walk in darkness for He is light.
We lie and tell not the truth, living
a sinful life that just ain't right.

But if we walk in the light as He is indeed the light,
we have fellowship one to another.
The blood of Jesus cleanses us from
all sin; His blood keeps us covered.

But if we say we have no sin, we
deceive ourselves and the truth is not in us.
If we confess our sins, He is faithful
to forgive us and clean us up.

If we say that we have not sinned we make
Him a liar and His word is not in us
(1Jo 1:10)

We Have an Advocate

John writes, my little children these things I
write unto you, that you sin not.
We have an advocate with the father
His Son, Jesus, the righteous, we've got.

We have the appeaser for our sins,
not just us but the sins of the world.
If you say you know Him, and do not keep His
Commandments, is throwing to swine, your pearls.

But those whosoever keep His word is
the Word of God perfected.
He that abides in Him ought to
walk as His walk projected.

He that said he is in the light and
hated his brother is in darkness even now.
He that loves his brother no matter what
walking in righteousness is your vow.

I write unto you, little children, because your sins
are forgiven you for His name's sake
(1Jo 2:12)

Love Not the World

Love not the world, neither the things
that are in the world, because if you do
any man who loves the world loves not the
Father, and the Father is not in you.

For the lust of the flesh, lust of the eyes, and
pride is the world, not the Father.
The world passes away and the lust thereof.
God's will takes us much farther.

Little children God's will abides forever.
Even now there are many antichrist that we know.
They went out from us, but not of us, the
antichrist will try to steal the Holy one's show.

Whoever denies the Son Jesus Christ
is antichrist, and he's a liar.
But he that acknowledges the Son has
also the Father, what more can we desire?

Whosoever denieth the Son, the same hath not the Father:
(but) he that acknowledgeth the Son hath the Father also
(1Jo 2:23)

Believe Not Every Spirit

Believe not every spirit, but try the spirits,
because many went out into the world.
Know you the spirit of God, for
the antichrist will make your head swirl.

Every spirit that confesses that Jesus is the
Christ and He has come in the flesh
is of God; he that confesses not
is not of God, but the antichrist mess.

Ye of God has overcome them, because
greater is He who is within you.
We are of God and He hears us,
hereby know that it is the spirit of truth.

Beloved know God and love.
And love ye one another.
He who loves not, knows not God,
Or His beloved Son, but loves the other.

No man hath seen God at any time. If we love one another,
God dwelleth in us, and His love is perfected in us
(1Jo 4:12)

Whosoever Believes

Whosoever believes that Jesus is born
of God and everyone who loves Him
knows by this love and keeps His
commandments which was given of them.

For, whosoever is born of God overcomes
the world, and this is the victory.
For if you believe that Jesus is the Son
of God, this certainly is no mystery.

This is He that came by water and blood,
even Jesus Christ not by water only.

Even by water and blood, the true spirit
of truth, cannot be taken wrongly.

For there are three that bear record in heaven,
the Father, the Word, and the Holy Ghost.
These three, yet they are One,
this marvelous Lord of Hosts.

He that has the Son hath life
(1Jo 5:12)

2 JOHN

The Second Epistle of John
For the Truth's Sake

For truth's sake which dwells in
us forever, grace be with you.
Grace, mercy, and peace, from God
and Jesus the Son, whose love is true.

No new Commandments do I write
but remind, of what we began with.
That we love one another in this life we
walk, for many deceivers can't do this.

They confess not that Jesus Christ has come in
the flesh, they are antichrist and deceive
Look to yourselves that we lose not the
things we've learned, then a full reward we'll receive.

Whosoever sins and lives not in the
doctrine of Christ has not the King.
He that lives in the teachings of Christ
has both the Father and Son, we have everything.

*If there comes any unto you, and brings not this doctrine,
receive him not... neither bid him God speed
(2Jo 10)*

3 JOHN

The Third Epistle of John
Greet Friends by Name

Beloved, follow not that which is
evil, but that which is good.
He that does good is of God, if you
are doing evil, you have truly misunderstood.

I wish above all that you prosper,
be in good health in body and soul.
I rejoiced greatly at your testimony that
the brothers you taught, taught what they were told.

I have no greater joy than to hear that
my children walk in truth.
For His name sake, they went forth urging
them to show hospitality that Diotrophes refused.

Demetrius hath good reports of all men
and of truth itself, and bears record.
We know that our record is true
and you have put in all the right effort.

... greet friends by name
(1Jo 3:14)

JUDE

Jude

Jude, brother and servant of Christ, and
the brother of James, had this to say.
Mercy, peace, and love be yours
but some have turned another way.

Beloved, I write to you of common salvation
that was once delivered to the Saints.
For certain men crept in unaware trying
to turn God's grace into what it ain't.

They deny that there was a Christ like those
delivered out of Egypt was destroyed for unbelief.
Even as Sodom and Gomorrha, sinful cities
suffering vengeance fire, for letting evil speak.

Woe to them that's gone the way of Cain
and ran greedily after sin's rewards.
Raging waves of foam out of shame
reserve the darkness and wandering stars.

These are murmurs and complainers
walking after their own lusts...
(Jud 16)

REVELATION

The Revelation of John
The Devine Introduction

This is a book of visions given to
John by God, of Christ's continual works.
John could see things to come of

heaven by means of gospel and church.

The revelation of Jesus Christ that God
showed him, which will shortly come to pass.
He sent His angel to signify it to John
and to keep us, until Jesus comes at last.

John bears record of the word of

God and our Lord Jesus' testimony.
Blessed is he who hears the word of

this prophecy, and knows it's not phony.

Keep those things that are written therein:
For the time is at hand.
John wrote to the seven churches
Grace and peace to you, I hope you too, understand.

Blessed is he that readeth and they that
hear the words of this prophecy...
(Rev 1:3)

Alpha and Omega, the Almighty

To the seven churches which are in Asia
Grace be unto you and peace,
from Him which is and which was
and which is to come, is of whom I speak.

From the seven Spirits which are before
His throne and who is the faithful witness.
The first begotten of the dead, the Prince of

Kings on Earth, whose love for us is the best.

He loves us and washed us from our
sins in His own precious blood.
He made us kings unto God, His father,
unto Him be the glory, and forever our love.

Behold, He comes with the clouds, and
every eye shall see Him, every eye.
All kindred of the earth, because of

Him shall wail, yes we shall cry.

I am Alpha and Omega, the beginning and the
ending said the Lord which was
and which is to come, the Almighty,
who covers us with His precious blood.

... even so, amen
(Rev 1:7)

He Reveled to John

He reveled to John a pure river of water
of life clear as crystal out of the throne of the lamb.
In the midst of it on the side was the tree
of life yielding fruit, serving the great I Am.

His servants shall serve Him, and they shall see
His face, and His name is on their foreheads.
There shall be no night or need of light,
for the Lord provides His light instead

Behold, I come quickly; blessed be he
that keeps the saying of this book.
I, John, saw these things and heard them,
then fell and worshipped at the angel's foot.

He then said unto me, do not do that, for I
am your fellow servant, worship God.

Seal not the saying of this book for the
time is at hand, go do your job.

He that is unjust, let him be unjust still.
He that is filthy, be filthy still.
He that is righteous and holy be ye still.
Your rewards are with Him, according to His will.

I shall give every man according to
his works, yes this shall be.
I Am Alpha and Omega, the first and the last.
Do His commandments and have a right to the tree.

Those who are not blessed are dogs and
sorcerers and whoremongers, and such,
liars, murderers, and idolaters, love to lie.
These sinners can't touch us.

I, Jesus, has sent my angels to testify
to you in the churches.
I Am the root and offspring of David,
The bright and morning star, only, worthy of worship.

And if any man shall take away for the words of the
book of this prophecy, God shall take away his part
out of the book of life, and out of the holy city, and
from the things which are written in this book
(Rev 22:19)

The grace of our Lord, Jesus Christ be with you all, Amen.